LEARNING TO UNDERSTAND
THE MISSION
OF THE
CHURCH

By Erland Waltner

Christian Service Training Series

FAITH AND LIFE PRESS, NEWTON, KANSAS

HERALD PRESS, SCOTTDALE, PENNSYLVANIA

Copyright © 1968 by Faith and Life Press, Newton, Kansas 67114,
and Herald Press, Scottdale, Pennsylvania 15683
Library of Congress Catalog Card Number: 68-59381
Printed in the United States of America

Foreword

Learning to Understand the Mission of the Church is the last of six courses in the Christian Service Training Series. The first five courses are: *Learning to Lead, Learning to Teach, Learning to Understand People, Learning to Know the Bible,* and *Learning to Work Together.*

The focus of this course is the nature and mission of the church. These two dimensions cannot be separated. The nature of the church requires that it be engaged in mission and helps to determine the character of that mission. Looked at from the other side, what the church does should be an expression of what the church is. It is the biblical view of the church which becomes decisive.

The basic purpose of this course is to aid growth in understanding of and participation in the life and work of the church. Understanding involves being able to see facts in their relationship to each other so that they have meaning and significance and find expression in behavior. This is particularly important in a time when the church is much misunderstood, sometimes misrepresented, and frequently subjected to rigorous criticism.

Beyond understanding, however, the concern is for growing participation in the witness and service of the church. The aim of this series is to help persons to participate in this ministry more freely, vigorously, intelligently, and effectively. Both greater freedom and greater competence in participation in mission are included in the objectives of this course.

The basic setting for this participation is the church in the world. This implies that Christians must also have some acquaintance with the kind of world in which they live, must know something of the depth of human lostness and frustration, and how disciples of Jesus Christ, individually and corporately, can helpfully live and serve in this world. A part of the course, therefore, has to do with the question of church-world relationships. The dilemma between being "in the world" but "not of the world" is faced and frankly explored.

The basic orientation reflects the Anabaptist-Mennonite background of the author and the anticipation that the material will be used primarily by those who stand in the same broad church tradition. However, the materials have drawn substantially on other than Anabaptist-Mennonite resources, and thus it is hoped that the course may also have significance for individuals and groups outside the denominational fellowship in which they have been produced. The commitment which the studies reflect, however, would be commonly recognized as belonging to the free church or the believers' church tradition.

The posture of this series is one of hope. The possibilities for the renewal and continued usefulness of the church in the hand of God underlie this study. While many persons are frustrated and discouraged about the present state of the church, both in its local and broader dimensions, this series of studies is based on the belief that renewal of the church is not only possible, but that God through His Holy Spirit is currently at work in many places both within as well as beyond the structures of the church. Participation in the church's mission of evangelism and service becomes a genuine expression of Christian hope.

The development of this course is thematic rather than expository. The outlines for *Learning to Understand the Mission of the Church* and the other courses in the Christian Service Training Series were prepared jointly by the Board of Education and Publication of the General Conference Mennonite Church, Newton, Kansas, and the Mennonite Commission for Christian Education of the Mennonite Church, Scottdale, Pennsylvania. In the process, the themes were assigned to the writer with suggestions concerning the purpose and content of each lesson. Leader's guides are also available.

Erland Waltner

Elkhart, Indiana
October 1968

Contents

Chapter 1

What Makes the Church Necessary?

> Why should men love the Church? Why should
> they love her laws?
> She tells them of Life and Death, and of all
> that they would forget.
> She is tender where they would be hard, and
> hard where they would like to be soft.
> She tells them of Evil and Sin, and other un-
> pleasant facts.
>
> —T. S. Eliot in "The Rock"[1]

In these penetrating lines, T. S. Eliot helps us to understand at least one reason why the church is being challenged in the modern world. Sometimes men attack the church because of its *faithfulness*. It is because men can scarcely bear to hear the witness of truth and righteousness and peace and salvation. Who wants to have his pretenses exposed or his favorite sins talked about?

This, however, can hardly be the whole story. Sometimes the *unfaithfulness* of the church is the reason for criticism. It is the failure of the church to be what God intended; or failure to do what Christ through His Holy Spirit is asking which is the reason for its ineffectiveness and for subsequent attacks.

It takes a great deal of wisdom to discern whether in a given instance the church is under fire because of faithfulness, or because of unfaithfulness. Superficial judgments on this question are not to be trusted. To probe more deeply into the question of what the church really is, what God intended the church to be, and in what ways the church in history and today has been faithful or unfaithful is one purpose for this study.

We need deeper understanding concerning the nature and mission of the church, concerning the task and message it has to proclaim, concerning the relation of the church to the world and how the church is to find expression in both the "gathered" and the "scattered" dimensions of its life. Where we find that the church is not living up to its highest potential, we want to know how the church can be renewed and how it may yet become more of that which the Lord intended.

Gaining a better understanding of the church, however, involves a risk. Better understanding in matters of Christian faith and fellowship always calls for something more. The outcome of our study is not to be merely the gathering of more information, or the experience of more dialogue, or the ability to explain to other people some of the things we have discussed. These lessons are intended to lead us "beyond understanding" into greater freedom and joy, deeper devotion and commitment, and more inspired and intelligent participation in the life and mission of the church. Samuel Shoemaker has taught us to pray, "Revive Thy church, O Lord, beginning with me."[2]

We start, however, with an elementary question. Is the church really necessary? And if so, why is it necessary? Even biblical scholars and theologians have argued about these questions. The answer depends on how we understand the nature and function of the church, how we discern basic human need in its spiritual dimensions, and how we read our Bibles in seeking to know God's mission (*missio Dei*) in the world.

The necessity of the church is not only something to talk about on Sunday morning when some members of the family may resist going to church. Nor is it pertinent only to the congregational meeting which discusses the question of whether or not to build a new church. Nor is it the province alone of the missions committee which struggles with the problem of church extension. The issue posed in this chapter is basic to the entire Christian enterprise.

While many are criticizing the organized church in the forms of expression in which it is found today, and while some are proposing a "churchless Christianity," our reading of the biblical materials supports the conviction that not only Christ but also His church must be taken seriously by anyone who considers himself in continuity with New Testament Christianity. Moreover, those who take seriously their denominational traditions, whether Anabaptist-Mennonite, main-line Protestant, or Roman Catholic, will be unable to escape the tremendous significance which the church has had in history.

WHAT IS THE CHURCH?

The Church Is People

Though volumes have been written on the nature and function of the church, it is necessary here to identify perspectives. By *church* we mean the Christian church as "the people of God in the world," the voluntary fellowship of believing, obeying, loving, witnessing, and serving people whose life and hope is in Jesus Christ.[3]

When we use the term *church* in a popular sense, it is common for us to think first of a building, as when we speak of the "Prairie Street Mennonite Church," or secondly, of an institution, organization, or denomination as when we speak of "the General Conference Mennonite Church," or thirdly, of a particular worship service as when we speak of "going to church." These popular usages of the term *church,* however, all fail to get at the essence of the nature and function of the church.

Through renewed study of the biblical concept of the church in various denominational study conferences in recent years, it has become clearer that according to the Bible the church is "primarily people, not buildings; primarily organism, not organization . . . it is fellowship rather than institution; it is togetherness and sharing rather than ecclesiasticism; it is participation in a common faith and a common life."[4]

The church then is a people. This is more than saying that the church consists of converted persons. It means that these persons, having entered into a new relationship with God through faith in Jesus Christ, are now also bound to each other in a community relationship. Entrance into this community is a voluntary act on

9

the part of each believer. However, at the center of the community is Jesus Christ who is its living Savior and its loving Lord. This lordship is exercised through the Holy Spirit. The church is to be found wherever Christ is, living and reigning, in the midst of His gathered people (Mt. 18:20), or abiding with and empowering His scattered people in their witness and service in the world (Mt. 28:19, 20).

The church then is the fellowship of believing persons. Their faith centers in Christ. It is the community of obeying persons. Their faith becomes action in response to their acknowledged Lord. It is the congregation of loving persons, whose relationships manifest the love of God shed abroad in human hearts through the Holy Spirit. It is the witnessing people, sharing among themselves and with others the good news of Jesus Christ. It is the serving people, who "in the name of Christ" minister to men in the depth of human need.

With Paul these people say, "For to me to live is Christ, and to die is gain" (Phil. 1:21). They are those who have been "born anew to a living hope through the resurrection of Jesus Christ from the dead" (1 Pet. 1:3). Their life and their hope is in Jesus Christ.

The Church Is Divine and Human

When we begin the task of attempting to identify or define the church, we might anticipate that this will be easy. The longer we study the Bible, however, and the more we reflect on the nature of the church, the more we become aware of its depth and complexity. In one sense, the church cannot be defined at all, and forever remains a kind of mystery. This is so because, according to Christian faith, the church has both a divine and a human dimension.

It is, on the one hand, the church of God, the product of God's own creative and redemptive work in the world. It is in this sense, always a working and manifestation of God's Holy Spirit breaking into human life and society. It shares the nature of mystery and miracle. It is completely dependent on the divine initiative.

10

On the other hand the church is also human, a sociological phenomenon. It is made up of human beings with all of their foibles and failings. It consists of people who have responded to the divine initiative and who are related to each other in this response to God's action in Jesus Christ through the Holy Spirit. Theologically, then, we may call it God's community of grace and discipleship, the fellowship of "sinners saved by grace," but it is also the community of "the saints striving after holiness." It is God's community of faith and love, the fellowship of believers, not just believing in anything but believing in Christ together. It is the brotherhood of *agape* love where each one bears the other's burdens and so fulfills the law of Christ.

The Church Is Universal and Local

The church understood in this way has both universal and local dimensions. The New Testament normally emphasizes the local visible congregation of believers as the particular and concrete expression of the church in a given place. It speaks of the church at Antioch, at Corinth, at Rome, and at other places. However, the New Testament also speaks of "the whole church" in Judea, Galilee, and Samaria (Acts 9:31). Especially in Colossians and Ephesians, the church is spoken of in a general and even universal sense. The idea of a local congregation and of the universal church are not in conflict with each other, but as Karl L. Schmidt puts it, "The Christian community in any particular place represents the whole body."[5] In this sense it is proper to emphasize the visibility of the church.

In attempting to understand the nature of the church, it is important that we recognize on the one hand the centrality of the local congregation as a concrete place where "the church happens." It is, in fact, the place where "the church can happen" with greatest frequency and regularity. This makes it an event of utmost seriousness when the local congregation comes together. On the other hand, the local congregation must always remember that while it represents the whole church, it is in itself not the whole church. Failing to be aware of this would be utter presumption.

11

The function of the church may be described in a variety of ways. Broadly, the function of the church may be viewed in terms of *what it is* and also in terms of *what it is to do.* Biblically, the church is not only the community of worship and learning but also the community of witness and service, proclaiming in word and deed the unsearchable riches of the Lord Jesus Christ and His full salvation. In fulfilling its function, it is the fellowship of the Great Commission: witnessing (Acts 1:8), evangelizing (Acts 4:20; 8:4), worshiping (Acts 2:47; Jn. 4:24; Eph. 5:19, 20), praying (Acts 4:24; 12:5), learning and teaching (Acts 2:42), assembling (Acts 2:46; Heb. 10:25), admonishing one another (Heb. 10:24, 25), ministering in love to each other (Acts 4:34; 11:29), and to the world (Gal. 6:10), thus fulfilling responsibilities to society and to the state (Rom. 13:1-7; 1 Pet. 2:13-17) as the salt of the earth and the light of the world (Mt. 5: 13-16). The church understood biblically is the continued corporate embodiment of the risen Christ, being in the world but not of the world, yet sent into the world to share in the mission of God.

Images and Functions

It is instructive to be aware of the many images which are used in the Bible to describe the church. One of these images is "the body of Christ." The meaning of this image is discussed in detail by Harold S. Bender in *These Are My People.* According to this image, the church is "the body" through which Christ continues to carry on His work. He is the Living Head of this body and members of the church are "the members of His Body."

Paul Minear in *Images of the Church in the New Testament* has called attention to the fact that there are over ninety images or analogies of the church in the New Testament.[6] Some of the more familiar ones are: the salt of the earth, the ark, the altar, the vineyard, the fig tree, God's planting, God's building, the bride of Christ, exiles and pilgrims, ambassadors, the people of God, the house of David, the Holy City, the holy temple, the light of the world, the household of God, the body of Christ. The fact that there are so many different images of the church should remind us that no one image should be pressed in all of its details, for each one is intended to illumine only some aspect of the nature of the church or of its function in the world. One element which many of these images have in common is that they suggest that the church is not an end in itself. It is intended to be a means through which God carries on His mission in the world. Biblically, then, the church is functional. It has a work to do.

Speaking more specifically of what the church is to do, we may recognize that on one side it has responsibilities to itself to become and to be that which God intends it to be. Here the functions of worship, fellowship, and nurture loom as deeply significant. These have to do with what Elizabeth O'Connor calls "the inward journey" of the congregational life.[7] No church can neglect these dimensions without losing its identity and power in the world.

On the other hand, the church also must make "an outward journey." Here the functions of witness and service are of utmost significance. The church which has no outreach is a contradiction in terms. Without proclamation, evangelism, prophetic witness, and social concern and ministry, the church becomes ingrown and sterile, and no longer partakes of the vitality or power of the church as we find it in the New Testament and in its creative periods in history.

Ministry of Reconciliation

If we seek for a single concept to express the central function of the church, we may with considerable confidence choose the expression "ministry of reconciliation." Biblically, this is expressed with clarity and power in 2 Corinthians 5:18-20: "All this is from God, who through Christ reconciled us to himself and gave us the ministry of reconciliation; that is, God was in Christ reconciling the world to himself, not counting their trespasses against them,

13

and entrusting to us the message of reconciliation. So we are ambassadors for Christ, God making his appeal through us. We beseech you on behalf of Christ, be reconciled to God."

Both the inward and the outward ministries of the ministering congregation partake of the nature of reconciliation. Whether we think in terms of the relationship to God, the relationship to a fellow believer, or the relationship to one who is outside the circle of faith and fellowship, the reconciliation which God has made possible in Jesus Christ is that which the church is to share.

WHY THEN IS THE CHURCH NECESSARY?

The Divine Mission

The church is necessary from the perspective of the divine mission in the world as this is revealed in the Bible. It is God's intention to create in this world a fellowship of redeemed and reconciled persons not only for the benefit and salvation of these persons, but for the benefit of the whole universe (Eph. 1; Rom. 8). While the church may take many different forms in the course of the changing circumstances and situations of history and while God is not limited to the organized church to do His work, yet according to Scripture God has chosen to work through persons in the context of a community of believing, loving, and serving people to fulfill His mission in the world.

For this purpose He brought the people of Israel into being, and for the fulfillment of this purpose He sent His Son, Jesus Christ, into the world. To continue His mission among the nations of the world, He has established through His Spirit the ongoing, living church of Jesus Christ.

Individual Need

The church is necessary from the perspective of the individual Christian. In a profound sense every individual Christian needs the Christian community. Normally, we do not become Christian apart from such a community, and we cannot become all that God intended us to be apart from the nurture, the admonition, the encouragement, the guidance, and support of the Christian community.

Deliberately to separate oneself from the church is spiritually suicidal. The old anecdote of the glowing coal which "went out" when it was separated from the other glowing coals, has truth in it. No Christian is "an island." Christians need each other in their worship, in their growth, in their search for the will of God, as well as in their witness and service for Christ in the world.

The World's Need

Finally the church is also necessary from the perspective of the world, though the world may not recognize this. In later lessons we will discuss a variety of meanings of the term *world* in the Bible. Meanwhile, thinking of "world" primarily as "mankind," we affirm that from the Christian perspective the church exists for the sake of this world. This is the world which God so loved that He gave His only begotten Son for its redemption.

The church is necessary to the world as a channel for an understanding of what God has done and is doing, and as a foretaste of that which He will yet do in establishing His kingdom. Without the church the world does not know that Jesus Christ is really Lord, not only of individual men, or only of the believing church, but also of society and its structures. Without the church the world does not understand the meaning of its own existence. Without the church the world gropes feverishly in its "lostness," reaching for that which it does not know or understand. When Jesus said to His followers, "You are the light of the world," and "You are the salt of the earth," He was affirming the necessity of the church for the sake of the world.

When the fullness of the kingdom of God has come, the church will no longer be necessary. Today it is still necessary.

1 T. S. Eliot, "Choruses from 'The Rock' " from *Collected Poems, 1909-1962* (New York: Harcourt, Brace and World, Inc.).

2 Samuel M. Shoemaker stresses the personal responsibility for renewal in his books, *By the Power of God* (New York: Harper, 1954), out of print, and *With the Holy Spirit and With Fire* (New York: Harper, 1960).

15

3 For a fuller statement on the nature and function of the church as seen from an Anabaptist-Mennonite perspective see Harold S. Bender, *These Are My People* (Scottdale, Pennsylvania: Herald Press, 1962).

4 Parts of this lesson are adapted from Erland Waltner, "The Church in the Bible," *The Believers' Church* (Newton, Kansas: Faith and Life, 1955), p. 70.

5 Karl Ludwig Schmidt, *The Church,* translated by J. R. Coates, (London: Adam and Charles Black, 1950), p. 66.

6 Paul S. Minear, *Images of the Church in the New Testament* (Philadelphia: Westminster Press, 1960).

7 Elizabeth O'Connor, *Journey Inward, Journey Outward* (New York: Harper and Row, 1968), pp. ix-x.

Chapter 2

How God Has Worked Through the Church

To speak of the church as the people of God in the world raises the question of when and how the church began and how God has worked among and through His people in history. This story is so vast and so many-sided that we can only include a few highlights in an account which biblically begins with Abraham and continues to the present moment. Even if all that is known would be included, the scope of the divine activity through the church is infinitely more extensive than has ever been recorded.

While it is traditional to speak of Pentecost (Acts 2) as the birthday of the church, it is important for us to see that the coming of Jesus into the world and the emergence of the Christian church as a recorded event are presented in the Bible as part of a larger and older context. The New Testament views the apostolic church as both in continuity and also in discontinuity with the Old Testament Israel. The church is continuous with Israel in that it continues to worship and serve the same God, responding to His calling and grace with the same quality of faith which Abraham had (Rom. 4). The church, however, also sees itself as a new creation (2 Cor. 5:14) primarily because of the newness which came into the world through Jesus Christ, the new Adam (Rom. 5). This paradox of the old and the new made it necessary for the early church to search out carefully what was to be retained and what was to be left behind. Such struggles as are reflected in the debates over circumcision (Acts 15), over the place of the law (Galatians), and over the old and the new priesthood (Hebrews), illustrate the tension between the old and the new in the emergence of the church as the new Israel.

We may speak of the Old Testament Israel as the church in preparation. This was the community of the old covenant, a family which became a nation, whose identity was determined by its response to the promise of God revealed and given to the patriarchs and the prophets of Israel.

A Covenant People

Basic to our understanding of the Old Testament community is the covenant. Not only was the covenant decisive in the relation of Abraham, Isaac, and Jacob to God, but it also became the basis for the blessing or judgment of Israel. Donald G. Miller has identified basic elements of the covenantal relationship which have implications for the ongoing life and work of the people of God.[1]

1. The covenant involved a relationship between a personal God and a nation of persons. God spoke to individual persons, such as Abraham, who responded in personal faith to His promises. It was not laws, ideas, or principles which were the basis of a covenant relationship, but personal encounter with a living God.

2. God took the initiative in the establishment of this covenant relationship. Men made the response. This continues to be the order in a saving covenantal relationship with God.

3. The covenant was grounded in God's mercy, not in the worthiness or the achievement of men. Israel came to be a "chosen" or "elect" people, not because of merit (Deut. 7:7, 8) any more than the Christian today can earn divine grace or salvation (Eph. 2:8).

4. God's gracious and mighty acts of redeeming love experienced by the people of Israel, as in the deliverance from Egypt, called for a response of gratitude, love, and obedience (Jer. 11:4; Ex. 24:7). So also God's redeeming love as we experience it in Jesus Christ evokes in us a response which is appropriate to that which has been done for us.

5. The response of obedience called for commitment to do the will of God as this was made known. It is not sufficient that the response be an inward feeling of thankfulness and joy, but

in a covenantal relationship, it requires outward action as well. When Israel's response became institutionalized and ritualistic, the prophets reminded the people that God was not pleased with their worship but that He required justice and righteousness (Amos 5:24). The social-ethical implications of the gospel of Christ are clearly required by the New Testament as well.

6. The concern of God was not only for the nation of Israel but for all nations. The covenant relationship with Israel therefore implied for the people a responsibility beyond Israel. While the grasp of Israel's universal mission in the world is not equally clear in all parts of the Old Testament, it is expressed strongly in such writings as Jonah and Isaiah. It is already recognized in Genesis 12:3 in the reference to the blessing which was to come to "all the families of the earth." It is made explicit in Isaiah 42:6, "I am the Lord, I have called you in righteousness . . . I have given you as a covenant to the people, a light to the nations. . . ," and in Isaiah 49:6, "I will give you as a light to the nations, that my salvation may reach to the end of the earth." On the basis of such passages, Georg Vicedom affirms, "The Bible in its totality ascribes only one intention to God: to save mankind."[2]

A Servant People

Recognizing that God's purpose for mankind is redemptive, the role of the nation of Israel is seen as that of a servant. It is basic to the idea of Israel as a "chosen people" that the whole people was to be involved in this servanthood. James Smart says, "The ministry of Israel belonged primarily and in principle to the nation as a whole. The basic meaning of Israel's existence was ministry, the service of God, the setting at God's disposal of human agencies through which He might work in order to effect the redemption of the world."[3]

In the unfolding history of Israel we perceive both achievement and failure, glory and shame. In the struggle of Israel to be the servant people of God, there emerged a variety of identifiable ministries, of which the best known are the prophetic, the priestly, and the kingly.[4] Especially in the earlier periods of the history of Israel, the three functions were at times combined in one person as in the case of Moses, Joshua, and even Samuel. At other times the functions were distributed and those who exercised them sometimes came into conflict with each other. Such conflict, however, represented a distortion and breakdown of the divine intention, for eventually in Jesus Christ all of these functions were integrated and fulfilled. The purpose of the ministering people of God in the Old Testament, frustrated as it was by the failure and disobedience of the people, ultimately found its fulfillment in the Servant of Servants, the Suffering Servant, Jesus Christ.

THE NEW TESTAMENT PEOPLE OF GOD

Jesus and the Church

New Testament scholars are not all agreed as to whether Jesus actually intended to establish the church and whether the references to the church in the Gospel of Matthew are to be considered authentic sayings of our Lord. Accepting the account of Matthew as trustworthy, however, we identify with those scholars who affirm that Jesus did intend to bring the church into being, even as He said to Peter, "On this rock I will build my church, and the powers of death shall not prevail against it" (Mt. 16:18). It is in the ministry, death, and resurrection of Christ that the church finds its ultimate source and the fountainhead of its being. It is of crucial importance that we see the ministry of Jesus in its wholeness rather than in fragmented form as is commonly done. To emphasize the importance of the death of Christ on the cross at the expense of His teaching ministry is a common error. To emphasize the significance of the resurrection of Jesus at the expense of His atoning death on Calvary is another common error. The Christ-event is in a profound sense a unit, and when we begin to break it apart analytically, trying to determine which part is of greatest importance, it is something like pulling the petals of a rose apart and thereby destroying the beauty and meaning of the whole. The gospel which Jesus preached and taught, the ministries of love which He rendered, the suffering and death which He experienced, and His resurrection from the dead together constitute a fabric of meaning which is lost unless it is seen in its wholeness.

Since in these lessons, however, we are concerned about the mission of the church, it is appropriate that we give particular attention to the ministry of Jesus. James Smart, with true insight, affirms, "The essential nature of the Christian ministry has been determined for all time by the ministry of Jesus Christ. All our thinking must take His person and ministry as its starting point."[5]

We note that Jesus identified His person and His ministry in response to "the servant of the Lord" passage from Isaiah 61 (Lk. 4:16-21). He identified Himself as the proclaimer of the gospel to the poor, as the friend of sinners, as "the Son of Man" who "came not to be served but to serve, and to give his life as a ransom for many" (Mk. 10:45).

James Smart sets out the following elements in the ministry of Jesus which have implications for our understanding of the ministry of the church for all time.

1. Jesus in His gospel, in His person, and in His ministry was completely consistent. Jesus always practiced what He preached. There is no incongruity between His character and His ministry.

2. Jesus in His ministry emphasized the proclamation of the kingdom of God. The *kingdom of God* is really a political figure of speech which means "the rule of God."

3. Jesus in His ministry was deeply concerned about the forgiveness of sins. He recognized that sin and the sense of guilt resulted in the brokenness of persons and estrangement in their relationships to God and men. He assured repentant sinners that they were forgiven, accepted by God even as Jesus had accepted them.

4. The ministry of Jesus took the posture of a servant. This was seen not only in His use of the "servant of the Lord" passages already mentioned, but also in the way He related to His disciples as well as to other persons. This relationship is much better symbolized by the pitcher, the basin, and the towel than it is by the

scepter, the crown, or the throne. Though He was Lord of all, He came as the servant of men (Phil. 2:7). The ministry of Jesus was carried on in a large variety of settings, sometimes involving large crowds, sometimes a family situation, and sometimes a one-to-one relationship.

Of special significance is the fact that in the course of His ministry, Jesus drew about Himself a circle of followers. The Gospel accounts agree that Jesus invited men to follow Him, literally to go with Him from one place to another in Palestine, and to become His disciples. The formation of this itinerant fellowship of disciples was a kind of preface to the emergence of the larger fellowship at the time of Pentecost (Acts 2). The invitation to join this circle of the disciples apparently was open to all who were willing to meet the conditions of repentance for sin and personal faith in Jesus. The number in the band of disciples apparently varied, for Luke at times speaks of the Twelve (Lk. 9:1), and again of "seventy others" (Lk. 10:1), and still later of "about one hundred and twenty" (Acts 1:15).

The Church in Acts and in the Epistles

The transition from the band of disciples which followed Jesus during His earthly ministry, to the apostolic church whose emergence is described in Acts 2, is a subject for deeper study than can be explored fully here. We note, however, that the church did not come into being with a constitutional convention, the adoption of a creedal statement, or the decision and mandate of some committee. Some have remarked, perhaps pessimistically, that if the birth of the Christian church had waited for committee action, it may well have been stillborn.

As we study the account of the emergence of the church given in Luke and Acts, we may note the following sequence:

1. Most important of all, there was an event: the coming, ministry, death, and resurrection of Jesus Christ, experienced by these early followers of the Lord.

2. Moreover, an interpretation of this event was given to the

apostles when their minds were opened to the meaning of Scriptures and they contemplated the relationship between what the Scripture said and what was happening in their experience (Lk. 24: 45-48; Acts 2:15-21).

3. To this event and the interpretation, they made a response of repentant and obedient faith (Acts 2:37-41).

4. They continued to gather as a group of believing disciples who were seeking to understand more fully the meaning of what had happened to them and to their Lord, whose visible presence had once been manifest but who now, though invisible, was still in their midst (Acts 2:42).

5. They continued to reflect on the meaning of their Lord's ministry and death and resurrection, and to instruct one another under the enlightenment of the Holy Spirit.

6. They began to bear witness to their experience and to their faith in the context of the new community which had been formed. Their witness was spontaneous and irrepressible. They said, "We cannot but speak of what we have seen and heard" (Acts 4:20).

Beyond telling us of the emergence of the apostolic church, the Book of Acts also gives an account of how the early church responded to opposition from without and unfaithfulness within. It tells of the persecution of the church in Jerusalem leading to a scattering and the spread of the Christian faith to other parts of Palestine, Asia Minor, Greece, and Italy. It portrays the "young church in action" (J. B. Phillips) with significant background information, helping us to understand letters written by Paul and other apostles. The Book of Acts together with the Epistles reveals not only how the Christian faith continued to spread but also how the Christian congregations developed their faith and life in various communities.

Some of these letters are concerned particularly about the return of Christ and the practical implications of this (1 and 2 Thess.). Some are concerned with questions of church unity, discipline, and worship practices (1 and 2 Cor.). Some are concerned with pastoral issues such as church organizations, dealing with false teach-

23

ings, and maintaining orthodox doctrine (the Pastoral Epistles). First Peter gives special encouragement to congregations of Asia Minor facing a hostile society and the prospects of strong persecution. Still others struggle with the transition from Jewish patterns of thought and life to the implications of Christian faith (Galatians, James, and Hebrews). Some have strong warnings against false teachings (1 John, 2 Peter, and Jude).

Careful formulations of Christian doctrine are found in Romans, Colossians, and Ephesians. These letters show that the early Christians knew they had a universal message to proclaim and a worldwide mission to perform. In Romans, Paul sees himself under "obligation both to Greeks and to barbarians, both to the wise and to the foolish" (Rom. 1:14). He declares himself eager to preach the gospel to those in Rome and he declares that it is the "power of God for salvation to every one who has faith, to the Jew first and also to the Greek" (Rom. 1:16). He develops the doctrine that all men need Christ, both Jews and Gentiles, and out of this emerges his strong compulsion to proclaim Christ where He has not already been named (Rom. 10:14-17; 15:20, 21).

The teaching of the universality of the church, however, is developed to the greatest degree in the letter to the Ephesians where in grand cadence and rich vocabulary the purpose of God to "unite all things" in Christ is projected as God's ultimate intention. In this the church, as the body of Christ (1:22, 23), has a vital and essential role (2:19-22; 3:7-13; 4:1-16) by recognizing, manifesting, and living out its oneness through the reconciliation which has been made possible through Jesus Christ.

THE CHURCH FROM APOSTOLIC TIMES TO THE REFORMATION

The fact that the church has continued to exist from biblical days to the present is one of the extraordinary realities of history. Roland Bainton, in *The Church of Our Fathers,* tells briefly and vividly the story of what has happened between the time of the Bible and our own day.[6] Neither his short resume' nor any other that we could include would do justice to the overwhelming record of important events which fill this period. Kenneth Scott Latourette quite properly describes it under the general title, *A History of the Expansion of Christianity* and fills six massive volumes with significant data.[7]

The Early Centuries

Repeated persecutions, the continuing spread of the Christian faith, the writing and gathering of the New Testament canon, the hammering out of early Christian doctrine, and the progressive organization of the ministries of the church characterized the opening five centuries.

By the fourth century, in the time of Constantine, Christianity formally became the religion of the Roman Empire, thus beginning a new era in its history. The development of the close ties between the church and the state, the growth of power centered in the bishop of Rome leading to the full-blown development of the office of the popes, the rise of monasticism and a sharp cleavage between clergy and the lay members of the churches, the division of the church into Eastern and Western segments—all these helped to usher in the so-called "dark ages" of the church in the medieval period. The Crusades led to the further shaping of doctrines supporting and exalting the power of the popes; and the abuses of these powers led to the rise of renewal groups such as the Cathari and the Waldenses in the twelfth century, the ministries of John Wycliffe in the fourteenth century, and of John Huss and Savonarola in the fifteenth century.

For those who are accustomed to think that nothing of God happened in the medieval period, it is good to recall that these were also centuries in which the Christian gospel came to northern Europe through such men as Patrick in Ireland, Martin in France, Boniface in Germany, and Ansgar the missionary to the Danes. It is also good to recall that these were the centuries when Christians like Francis of Assisi lived and taught, Thomas a Kempis wrote the *Imitation of Christ,* and John Wycliffe initiated the translation of the Holy Scriptures into English.

The Reformation as Renewal

The Reformation which began in the early part of the sixteenth century is generally interpreted by Protestants as a major renewal movement in the church. With Martin Luther considered the most vigorous leader, such men as Zwingli, Menno Simons, John Calvin, Beza, John Knox, Latimer, and Cranmer are generally counted among the leading reformers. Roland H. Bainton characterized the Reformation as a movement "back to the Bible." One of its basic slogans was that the Bible, rather than the pope or the tradition of the church, was to be the authority for the church's faith and practice. Under the sway of the vigorous preaching and teaching of the Bible by the reformers, masses of people broke away from the Church of Rome and began to move in the direction of modern Protestant denominationalism.

Within the larger ferment of the reform movements, were the Anabaptists who agreed with the main-line reformers on many things but who also differed with them because they felt that the Reformation was not moving rapidly enough or going far enough.[8] Particularly objectionable to the Swiss Brethren was the readiness of Zwingli to leave the decision concerning the propriety of infant baptism in the hands of the Zurich City Council. Having become convinced that infant baptism is unscriptural and that political authorities should have no jurisdiction over matters of Christian faith, the Swiss Brethren broke away from the Zwinglian movement and became a part of what some have called "the left wing of the Reformation." Suffering intensely for their faith at the hands of both Roman Catholics and other Protestants, the Anabaptist brethren left to their spiritual descendants and to the world a rich heritage of courage, faith, and piety.

FROM THE REFORMATION UNTIL THE PRESENT

A Rich Legacy

The Protestant Reformation, of which the Anabaptist movement may be considered a distinct part, has left to the contemporary church and world a rich legacy. The rediscovery of the Bible and its significant place in the life of Christians, the emphasis on salvation by grace through faith, and the universal priesthood of all believers are abiding values. Moreover, special contributions made by the Anabaptist wing of the Reformation include the following concepts: 1) that the church is a voluntary fellowship of believers separate from the state, 2) that the Christian life is to be one of obedient discipleship under the lordship of Christ, and 3) that this involves a commitment to the love-ethic of Jesus, including love of personal and national enemies.[9]

Signs of Trouble

Honest scrutiny of the church in the world today, however, discloses quickly that things are not as they ought to be. Christendom in a traditional sense is breaking down, and historians speak of a transition being made into a "post-Christian era." The church in the world, divided into hundreds of separate denominational bodies, finds itself in trouble. Voices from within the church and from without are calling for a new reformation.

Some of the great strengths of Protestantism have developed some weaknesses. The emphasis on a universal and direct priesthood of all believers, as over against the papal system, has given rise not only to denominationalism but also to a high degree of local congregationalism and individualism in matters of Christian faith. This has destroyed to a large extent the organizational unity of the church and has made difficult any form of spiritual unity. The emphasis on the authority of Scripture has led to varying interpretations concerning the nature of this authority and to various doctrines of the inspiration of the Bible, as is illustrated in the fundamentalist-modernist controversies of former decades and in the neoorthodox, neoliberal, and neofundamentalist discussions of more recent times. The emphasis on salvation by faith alone has left serious gaps in the area of Christian social responsibility and thus has opened the way for tensions between those who champion the cause of evangelism as the primary task of the church and those who are pressing social concerns such as peace, racial justice, and the conquest of poverty.

Some feel that the church is hopelessly irrelevant to modern issues and has lost its power to communicate the gospel to contemporary man. There are, however, signs of hope and a manifest working of God's Spirit in the contemporary church. These will be discussed in the last two chapters. We may be confident that God does not leave Himself without a witness in any generation, including our own.

1 Donald G. Miller, *The Nature and Mission of the Church* (Richmond: John Knox Press, 1957), pp. 33-44.

2 Georg F. Vicedom, *The Mission of God* (St. Louis: Concordia, 1965), p. 4.

3 James Smart, *The Rebirth of Ministry* (Philadelphia: Westminster Press, 1960), p. 49.

4 *Ibid.*, p. 43.

5 *Ibid.*, p. 18.

6 Roland Bainton, *The Church of Our Fathers* (New York: Charles Scribner's Sons, rev. ed., 1950).

7 Kenneth Scott Latourette, *A History of the Expansion of Christianity* 6 vols. (New York: Harper, 1944). Out of print.

8 Cf. Cornelius J. Dyck, ed., *An Introduction to Mennonite History* (Scottdale, Pennsylvania: Herald Press, 1967), especially Chapters 1 and 2.

9 Harold S. Bender, "The Anabaptist Vision," reprinted in Guy F. Hershberger, ed., *The Recovery of the Anabaptist Vision* (Scottdale, Pennsylvania: Herald Press, 1957). This was originally given as the presidential address of the American Society of Church History in December 1943.

Chapter 3

Understanding the Task of the Church

Life magazine several years ago pictured a gadget which had been built by a creative gadgeteer. It had a variety of wheels and sprockets with fitting belts and chains. It ran economically. It was efficient. But it served no conceivably useful function. It was simply an interesting gadget. Is this a symbol of the contemporary church, with its wheels and its motions? What useful thing does the church really do? What ought it do? What is its task?

If anything has become clear in recent studies of the church, it is that the church of Christ, to be true to the divine intention, must be involved in mission. There is really no participation in Christ without participation in His mission.

While there are various ways of stating the mission of the church, one of the best ways, a biblical way, is to speak of it as a ministry of reconciliation. As was indicated in chapter one, this is best expressed in 2 Corinthians 5:18-20.

The Ministry of Reconciliation

Arnold Come, in his book, *Agents of Reconciliation,* focuses attention on this way of perceiving and describing the Christian task.[1] He uses the title of his book to describe in a comprehensive way his conception of the Christian mission. Calvin Redekop in an essay, *The Church Functions with Purpose,* lists reconciliation as the first function of the church. He also lists the ministry of love, discernment, admonition, and transmission of the faith as other functions. In a broad sense, however, these could also be comprehended as dimensions of reconciliation. Reconciliation in this comprehensive sense includes both the experience of being reconciled and the task of helping others to be reconciled.[2] Reconciliation means "redemption, restoration, the establishment of a new relationship." According to Webster's dictionary, reconciliation means "to restore to friendship, harmony, and communion." This presupposes an estrangement, an alienation, a broken relationship. Biblically, this alienation is a manifestation and consequence of sin. Reconciliation is at the heart of the meaning of the term *salvation.*

Reconciliation in Three Dimensions

Pierre Widmer, Mennonite pastor and educator of Grand-Charmont, France, explains that the ministry of reconciliation as a Christian task involves at least three dimensions: 1) the reconciliation of God and man, where alienation has come because of human sin; 2) the reconciliation of man with himself, since human sinfulness also estranges man from himself causing conflict within his own being; and 3) the reconciliation of man with his fellow men from whom he is alienated by all that sin does to blight, frustrate, and destroy harmonious human relationships.[3]

Biblically conceived, however, reconciliation is not only a concept which looks backward, it also looks forward. Come properly recognizes that "reconciliation consists of nothing short of the restoration and fulfillment of God's original and persistent purpose for His creation."[4] The goal of the reconciling work of God is not merely a "return to union," but it is a movement toward the realization of man's eternal destiny with God. It is not simply the recovery of a lost status, but it is a movement toward a glorious fulfillment of all that God intended man to be.

The theme of reconciliation is deeply embedded in the entire Bible. In the Old Testament (Ex. 3:7, 8) Moses recognized the redeeming and reconciling work of God in the experience of Israel being delivered from the Egyptian bondage. When Israel in the course of history through disobedience was again and again estranged from God, its spiritual leaders, especially the prophets, called the people to return in repentance to faithfulness to the covenant relationship so that they might experience forgiveness and restoration.

The prophet Micah saw, however, that reconciliation and peace were intended for all nations, and he spoke of the day when the nations would come to Mount Zion to hear God's Word and to learn His ways:

> . . . and they shall beat their swords into plowshares,
> and their spears into pruning hooks;
> nation shall not lift up sword against nation,
> neither shall they learn war anymore;
> but they shall sit every man under his vine
> and under his fig tree,
> and none shall make them afraid;
> for the mouth of the Lord of hosts has spoken.

Micah 4:3, 4

Isaiah in his perception of God's ultimate reconciling purpose, sees that this goes even beyond the human race when he says,

> The wolf shall dwell with the lamb . . .
> and a little child shall lead them. . . .
> The sucking child shall play over the hole of the asp. . . .
> They shall not hurt or destroy in all my holy mountain;
> for the earth shall be full of the knowledge of the LORD
> as the waters cover the sea. Isaiah 11:6, 8, 9

The Reconciler

This glorious vision of God's plan of love and peace in a world where men live in a relationship of reconciliation, though it has been frustrated by human sin through the ages, is reaffirmed in the New Testament. Both in His earthly ministry and in His exaltation as the risen Lord, Jesus Christ is seen as the Reconciler and the Prince of Peace. In sending Christ into the world, God was providing a way for the reconciliation of the world to Himself (2 Cor. 5:19). Not only did Jesus teach that human relationships are to be controlled by the spirit of forgiving and reconciling love (Mt. 5:24; 6:38-48; Lk. 6:27-36; Mt. 18:21-35), but He also imparted to His followers the legacy of His peace saying, "Peace I leave with you; my peace I give to you; not as the world gives do I give to you. Let not your hearts be troubled, neither let them be afraid" (Jn. 14:27). On the cross He prayed in the spirit

31

of forgiving love, "Father, forgive them; for they know not what they do" (Lk. 23:35).

Interpreting the meaning of Christ's suffering and death, Paul writes to the Colossians concerning Christ saying, "For in Him all the fulness of God was pleased to dwell, and through him to reconcile to himself all things, whether on earth or in heaven, making peace by the blood of his cross" (Col. 1:19, 20).

In the letter to the Ephesians, the reconciling work of Christ is described in exalted terms:

> In him we have redemption through his blood,
>   the forgiveness of our trespasses,
> according to the riches of his grace
>   which he lavished upon us.
> For he has made known to us in all wisdom and insight
>   the mystery of his will, according to his purpose
> which he set forth in Christ as a plan for the fulness of time,
>   to unite all things in him,
> things in heaven and things on earth. Ephesians 1:7-10

This is not simply a goal to be contemplated, but is already a part of the experience of the Christian community. In Ephesians 2, he describes how men who were once "dead through trespasses and sins" have now been "made alive" in Christ and established in a saving and serving relationship to God and man. He speaks of the Gentiles, having been alienated both from God and from the Jewish community, who "now in Christ Jesus . . . have been brought near in the blood of Christ. For he [Jesus] is our peace, who has made us both one, and has broken down the dividing wall of hostility" (Eph. 2:13, 14). This reconciliation experienced by the Christian community through Christ is both a model and foretaste of that which God in principle seeks to bring about in the world.

The Messianic Shalom (Evangelism and Peace)

Another way of stating the task of the church is to say that it is to be a witness to and an embodiment of the messianic *Shalom*. *Shalom* is the Hebrew word for peace. J. C. Hoekendijk, in analyzing the evangelistic task of the church, summarizes it on the basis of three great words, *kerygma, koinonia, and diakonia.*[5]

1. The *Shalom* is proclaimed. This is *kerygma* which means "the spoken proclamation." This is evangelism by the spoken word whether from the pulpit or in a face-to-face situation.

2. The *Shalom* is lived. This is *koinonia* which means "fellowship." *Konionia* in the New Testament sense means living the reconciled life together in Jesus Christ.

3. The *Shalom* is demonstrated. This is *diakonia* which means "service." The term emphasizes the idea of humble ministry focused on meeting real human need, whether that need be physical, emotional, or intellectual.

To speak of the church's task as a ministry of reconciliation or to speak of it as the proclamation and embodiment of the messianic *Shalom*, is, in effect, to say the same thing. In each case, however, we must avoid the false antithesis which is commonly set up between the church's task of evangelism and the Christian's task of social action. In the ministry of Jesus, these two dimensions of His redeeming and reconciling mission were not separated. Jesus ministered to the total needs of men, spiritual, emotional, and physical. This is well illustrated in the healing of the paralytic who was carried to Jesus by his four friends (Lk. 5:17-26). Likewise, in the ministry of the early church so aptly illustrated in the healing of the lame man at the gate of the temple (Acts 3:1-10), the apostles were concerned about responding to the man's total need. Functionally, as an application of the principle of division of labor (Acts 6:1-6), the early church did set apart some persons to be especially responsible for preaching and others to be responsible for the serving of tables. This, however, was a process of internal organization in which the church, recognizing gifts and previous experience with the Lord, made an arrangement by which total responsibilities might be discharged.

Functionally, we may in the church distinguish between the various types of ministries as the New Testament also does (Rom. 12:3-8; 1 Cor. 12:4-11, 27-30; Eph. 4:11). However, the variety of functions converge in what is essentially *one mission.*

Attempts which have arisen in our time to exalt one or another aspect of the church's mission are to be viewed with concern. It is imperative from the New Testament perspective that each be seen in the context of the whole. Operationally, too, it is wise to keep the witnessing and the helping functions in the church's ministry close to each other. Each is necessary to give the other clear Christian meaning and effectiveness.

The Christian task in the ministry of reconciliation cannot be fulfilled until the whole of Christ has been brought to bear on the whole need of man. The arena for this reconciling ministry is the whole world with no race, class, creed, or nation excluded from the gamut of Christian responsibility.

THE LOCAL CONGREGATION IN THE MINISTRY OF RECONCILIATION

To speak of the Christian task in such large and general terms may tempt us to be overwhelmed and to consider it out of reach for us, and to leave that responsibility to our denominational leaders. We must, therefore, recognize that the local congregation of which we are a part is the locus of our own basic responsibility for this ministry of reconciliation.

Levels of Church Life

We may note here that the church exists on various levels.

1. One now familiar form is the small group, sometimes called "the *koinonia* group," made up of from two to twelve persons who relate to each other as fellow believers in a regular and intimate way. The Christian family, itself, may be one form of a *koinonia* group.

2. A second familiar form is the local congregation, which varies considerably in size from one community to another, but generally consists of persons living in the same geographical locality so that members may gather regularly for their meetings of worship, instruction, fellowship, and decision-making.

3. A third level is that of the denominational conference, made

up of representatives of various congregations, generally located in a larger geographical region, or perchance, as representatives of congregations or of regional conferences meeting on a national level.

4. A fourth extension of the conference level is the world church, whether it meets as a "council of churches" with ecumenical representation from the various countries of the world or in an international denominational framework as the Mennonite World Conference.

5. A fifth level is the church-related institution or agency which may be an extension of a local congregation, a regional group of congregations, a denomination, or even a group of denominations. In function, it may be educational (school), rehabilitating (hospitals), custodial (homes), or it may exist as a service agency such as the Mennonite Central Committee, Mennonite Research Agency, or Mennonite Mutual Aid.

Calvin Redekop has helpfully observed that not all of the functions of the church can be carried on with equal effectiveness at all levels of church life and organization. In focusing on the man-to-man dimension of the ministry of reconciliation, he notes that this can be best experienced and shared at the level of the small group or possibly the small congregation. In its most authentic form, he says, reconciliation takes place in "primary type groups," that is, in those "in which relationships are face-to-face, intimate, and lasting."[6] He suggests that "reconciliation takes place in inverse proportion to the size of the group." The implications of this for church meetings and church organization need to be explored further.

Our basic concern here is not the size or the type of the group, but the fact that it is precisely in the context of our primary relationships, in the home, in the small group, in the local congregation, in the neighborhood, or at the job that "the ministry of reconciliation" must begin. Before we can go to the "ends of the earth" with this glorious message of reconciliation and peace, our primary relationships need to be examined. Here any honest appraisal will disclose the need for an active and continuing recon-

35

ciling ministry. It does not necessarily follow that we cannot minister anywhere else if we do not have perfect reconciliation in the local group. To insist on perfection at home before we can serve abroad would paralyze the Christian mission at once and restrict it tragically. Neither the apostles nor the early church was perfect, yet God worked then as He does now through imperfect persons and imperfect groups.

The force of the above concern, however, must not be lost. It is as the local congregation becomes a true community of reconciled and reconciling persons, whether through small *koinonia* (fellowship) groups or by some other work of the Holy Spirit, that it may then become a viable model and a vital force for reconciliation in the larger community and in the world. Much of the failure of the church's witness is due to its failure to be a reconciled and reconciling community at the local level.

Basic to the experience of reconciliation is the necessity of forgiveness. William Klassen has elaborated the need for the church to become "the forgiving community." This imperative rests on solid biblical grounds, as Klassen has demonstrated, and also finds strong support in the observations and experience of contemporary psychiatry.[7]

Worship and the Word

A variety of activities in addition to the meeting of persons in small group situations are needed to help the local congregation to become a reconciled and reconciling community. Many of the traditional activities of the church find their validation in the fact that they are necessary to provide a climate and setting in which meaningful personal encounters leading to reconciliation can take place.

Basic are the activities which make up the worship and nurture functions of the local congregation. Far from being a dispensable activity, gatherings for the purpose of corporate worship become an essential dimension of the church's ministry. Eduard Schweizer, in a careful study of *Church Order in the New Testament,* says,

"There can be no doubt that to a great extent worship is the center of the church's life."[8] Gerhard Delling in his definitive study of *Worship in the New Testament* affirms that "worship is in its essence a self-portrayal of the congregation."[9] Norman E. Richardson affirms "Public worship is the church's primary function. . . . Worship is the means whereby the sense of the living Presence of God is kept alive within the church." William Nicholls even more strongly affirms, "Worship is the supreme and only indispensable activity of the Christian church. It alone will endure, like the love for God which it expresses, into heaven, when all other activities of the church will have passed away."[10]

Moreover, the *searching out* and the *interpretation* of the Word of God as it is given to the church in the Scriptures is likewise essential. How shall the fruits of the gospel be manifest in the life of the congregation unless the roots of congregational fellowship are nourished deeply and richly in the Scriptures. This also calls for *discernment,* the diligent search for the implications of the meaning of the gospel for each situation, not only by an appointed minister but by the entire congregation. Moreover, it calls for *admonition* as some members begin to see new light which other members do not yet see or having seen do not yet follow. The *instruction, counseling,* and *care* of every member of the fellowship, some of whom are children, youth, the sick, the bereaved—and those in all age groups who may have specialized kinds of needs—all become part of the concern of a local congregation which takes the ministry of reconciliation seriously and seeks to apply it as widely as possible. In a later lesson, the life and work of the "gathered church" will be discussed in greater detail.

THE EXTENSION OF MINISTRY BEYOND THE LOCAL CONGREGATION

If the church's ministry in the world were limited to that which a local congregation or a small group can do, it would be severely restricted. Local congregations, however, may join forces with other congregations in order to undertake ministries which they would be unable to accomplish alone. This is the functional basis for the church in the form of a conference organization or in the form of a service agency or an institution. Even brief reflection will bring to mind a large number of ministries which may be undertaken only on a supracongregational level. They can be most efficiently and effectively done when more than one congregation participates. A local congregation which has grown numerically and spiritually strong may undertake to plant a new congregation somewhere near its own location. However, when the need arises, as it frequently does, to establish a new congregation at some considerable geographical distance from the existing local congregations, whether this be in the homeland or in an overseas situation, it is often better to do this through a conference service agency such as a mission board. Likewise, the administration of relief ministries, whether in situations caused by war or by natural disasters, particularly when some geographical distance is involved, calls for some kind of relief agency.

The education of youth, particularly at the levels of higher Christian education and the preparation of persons for various congregational and denominational ministries calling for specialized skills and training, requires more resources in finances, in facilities, in faculty and staff, and in program planning than can normally be undertaken by a small group or a local congregation. The same applies to the writing, editing, publishing, printing, and distribution of Christian literature whether for evangelistic, educational, or more general purposes. This exceedingly important avenue of Christian ministry, also a facet of the ministry of reconciliation, can best be done through a well-supported and well-developed church-related publishing house or some similar agency. Various kinds of hospitals for persons in physical or emotional distress, and various kinds of homes, whether for the aged or for homeless children or others needing special care, are sometimes developed on a local level. Seldom is a single local congregation able to carry the full responsibility for such an institutional ministry.

Church institutions and service agencies, then, are involved in the larger ministry of reconciliation. Their place in this ministry is more specialized than that of a local congregation. Institutions may differ widely from each other because of the particular type of function which they are designed to serve.

Agencies and Congregations

The effectiveness of the ministry of church institutions depends on at least two kinds of conditions. On the one hand, institutions and agencies must not lose sight of their relationship to local congregations and to the conferences which they represent in a specialized ministry. They must remain conscious of how their special function is but one part of a larger ministry of reconciliation.

One of the frequent tragedies in the history of the church institutions and agencies is the development of a wide gap between them and the congregations. Whenever this happens, the situation itself calls for a ministry of reconciliation. Even as Christians in the local congregation are to be concerned about reconciliation with persons in a primary group, so those who lead and serve institutions and those who lead and serve congregations must be concerned about maintaining open lines of communication and reconciled brotherly relationships.

The other side of the coin, however, is the fact that congregations need to recognize that they need institutions and agencies to fulfill their part in the total ministry. For members of a local congregation to limit themselves to their own internal concerns, or even to limit their witness and service to the immediate community in which the congregation is located, is to develop a nearsighted view of the Christian mission and thereby to restrict and frustrate the larger witness of the church in the world.

This larger ministry through conference agencies and institutions requires the dedicated support in prayer, counsel, finances, and persons on the part of local congregations. The agencies and institutions are but the arm of the local congregations. But arms need to be fed by the lifeblood of the body if they are to perform the functions for which each of them has been established.

Honest Reevaluation of Structures

It follows that from time to time the supporting congregations, the sponsoring conferences, and the agencies and institutions themselves need to ask whether the intended functions are being carried out in the best possible way. Especially in an age of rapid change, agency and institutional structures, as well as congregational structures, may become obsolete and may outlive the needs for which they were set up. New needs call for new structures. The change and even the abandonment of structures may become necessary in order to keep the church's ministry contemporary. It is possible that what was once a dire human need to which the church was led of the Holy Spirit to respond is now being met by some other agency such as the civic community or the state. Since human need always seems to exceed the church's material resources, it is necessary to take inventory from time to time to see whether the church's resources are being used effectively.

When change and even the abandonment of old structures is seen to be the verdict of wisdom, such change must be undertaken with the same kind of courage and dedication which was called for in the initiation of these structures. It is not altogether surprising that the abandonment of structures is often more difficult and painful than their establishment.

By what criteria should Christians evaluate the various kinds of ministries which are being carried on and which are possible? Charles Feilding suggests at least four basic questions which ought to be raised: 1. In what way does it communicate the gospel? 2. Is it a ministry of the church and not merely a private venture? 3. Does it exhibit the respect for persons required by the Christian faith? and 4. Is it directed toward the surrounding world and culture in a manner worthy of a body set in the world to be its light and the agent of God's will for the unity of all?[11]

1 Arnold B. Come, *Agents of Reconciliation* (Philadelphia: Westminster Press, rev. ed., 1964).

2 Calvin Redekop, *The Church Functions with Purpose* (Scottdale, Pennsylvania: Herald Press, 1967), pp. 9-20.

3 Pierre Widmer, "The Holy Spirit and Reconciliation," *The Witness of the Holy Spirit*, Proceedings of the Eighth Mennonite World Conference, Amsterdam, The Netherlands, July 23-30, 1967 (Elkhart, Indiana: Mennonite World Conference, 1967), pp. 88-92.

4 Come, *op. cit.*, p. 29.

5 J. C. Hoekendijk, *The Church Inside Out* (Philadelphia: Westminster Press, 1966), p. 25.

6 Redekop, *op. cit.*, pp. 21, 22.

7 William Klassen, *The Forgiving Community* (Philadelphia: Westminster Press, 1966), especially Chapter X, "The Church as a Forgiving Community."

8 Eduard Schweizer, *Church Order in the New Testament* (Naperville, Illinois: Alec R. Allenson, Inc., 1961), p. 220.

9 Gerhard Delling, *Worship in the New Testament* (Philadelphia: Westminister Press, 1962), p. xiii.

10 William Nicholls, *Jacob's Ladder: The Meaning of Worship* (Richmond): John Knox Press, 1958), p. 9.

11 Charles Feilding, "Education for Ministry" published in *Theological Education*, Autumn 1966, p. 81.

Chapter 4

Clarifying the Message of the Gospel

In the *Expository Times* of August 1967, H. J. Hamerton of Leeds, England, has an article entitled *"Preach the Gospel to Every Creature,"* in which he pleads that kindness to animals is a form of preaching the gospel. He says, "When God's love is mediated to animals, a genuine preaching of the Gospel takes place." In a critical response to this article in *Church Growth Bulletin,* Donald McGavran declares that he too believes in "kindness to animals, the battle for brotherhood, and more Christian economic relationships between labor and capital," but adds, "in the interest of clarity, we doubt the wisdom of calling all these good deeds 'preaching the Gospel.' . . . Let us have no more of this *non*sense, my dear friends, my very dear friends."[1]

INTELLIGENT WITNESS NEEDED

The above dialogue illustrates the need to clarify the message which the church has to proclaim. On the surface it would appear that our task is to define with precision the *content* of the gospel. This, we say, is the function of theology, namely, to reflect on and to clarify the Christian faith.

The basic biblical passage for this series of lessons, in 2 Corinthians 5:19, says that the church has been entrusted with "the message of reconciliation." To think through this message carefully so that we may be able to articulate it clearly is, however, not only the responsibility of the theologian and of the preacher, but it is also the responsibility of every believer. Each of us should be able to bear intelligent witness to our faith and to give "a reason of the hope" that we profess (1 Pet. 3:15). In a nonprofessional sense, every Christian is a theologian, that is, one who thinks concerning his faith. We may, with certain proprieties, speak of "the theologianhood of all believers."[2] The truth is that many of us already claim this role in any case, since we make judgments concerning our professional theologians and our preachers and teachers as to whether they are true to the gospel. Some, to be sure, think on Christian faith more clearly, and others in a more confused manner.

Medium and Message

Lest we oversimplify the task of clarifying the message of the church, we do well to reflect on the meaning of a contemporary slogan by Marshall McLuhan that "The medium is the message."[3] McLuhan is speaking primarily of modern technological mass media, such as television, in which he believes the medium is its own message. But, come to think of it, is this not also profoundly true of the Christian message?

We read, "God was in Christ reconciling the world to himself" (2 Cor. 5:19). "In the beginning was the Word, and the Word was with God, and the Word was God. . . . And the Word became flesh and dwelt among us" (Jn. 1:1, 14). "For in him all the fulness of God was pleased to dwell" (Col. 1:19). "For he is our peace" (Eph. 2:14). These passages remind us that Jesus Christ was both the medium by which God ultimately communicated to men and that He was Himself the message which was being communicated. In the case of Jesus Christ, too, then "the medium is the message." This in turn has profound implications for our thinking concerning the nature of the Christian message and the way that it is to be communicated in the world. In the case of God's communication to men, the medium is a person, not a machine, not even ultimately a book, but a living human being who shared the joys and sorrows of men.

Jesus Is Lord

In this lesson it is not possible to examine all that the church believes or proclaims. We can focus on only one central affirmation of faith which was basic in the early church and which continues to have profound meaning for the church today, namely, the confession that "Jesus is Lord."

A Mennonite New Testament scholar, Vernon Neufeld, in a doctoral study on early Christian confessions, has examined various formulations of how the early church identified Jesus. Basic are the following:

Jesus is Christ (John 1:20; 1 John 2:22, 5:1)
Jesus is Lord (Romans 10:9; Philippians 2:11)
Jesus is Son of God (John 1:34; 1 John 4:15)

In the sermon of Peter on the Day of Pentecost, according to Acts 2:36, he declared, "That God has made him both Lord and Christ, this Jesus whom you crucified." Here two of the titles applied to Jesus are brought together. Neufeld holds that the confession, "Jesus is Christ," is the earliest form, basing this on Peter's confession at Caesarea Philippi (Mk. 8:29), and Jesus' own acknowledgement of His person during His trial (Mk. 14:61, 15:2). However, in all three of the basic forms of this early confession, employing the terms Christ, Lord, and Son of God, is involved "the predication of a more than ordinary nature and function expressed by the title given to Him." In these confessions, Neufeld affirms, is represented "the basic core of the Christian faith." The term *Christ* not only recalled the messianic expectations and affirmed their true fulfillment in Jesus, but also acclaimed Him as "the One who suffered death and who also experienced the resurrection." The expression *Son of God* affirmed the conviction "that Jesus is the unique Son of the Father . . . the only Mediator between God and man." The term *Lord* not only set Jesus over against the lordship of Caesar, but in its broadest sense affirmed that Jesus is "the Lord of the Christian servant, the Lord of the assembled congregation, and, indeed, the Lord of all."[4]

The fact that all of these early confessions used the name *Jesus* is of equal significance, for this is clearly intended to identify the historical human Jesus of Nazareth, who experienced the trials and tribulations of men, even as other men experienced them. This early Christian creed affirms concerning Jesus Christ, with equal emphasis, that He was human and that He was more than human. The danger of neglecting either the humanity or the deity of Jesus Christ in the proclamation of the Christian faith is well illustrated in the development of Christian thought in the history of the church.

In many passages in the New Testament, the term *Savior* is likewise applied to Jesus, sometimes in connection with one of the other titles (Lk. 2:11; Jn. 4:42; Tit. 1:4; 2:11; 3:6). In 2 Peter the appellation is enlarged to "our Lord and Savior Jesus Christ" (2 Pet. 1:11; 2:20; 3:18).

We Preach Jesus Christ

In short, then, the church believes and proclaims that Jesus Christ is Savior and Lord, fully human and fully divine, and that His coming, His teaching, His death, His resurrection and ascension, and His coming again have implications for the meaning of history, for the individual believer, for the life of the church, and, indeed, for the whole world. Of the early apostles it was said simply that they preached "Jesus as the Christ" (Acts 5:42), or that they proclaimed "the Christ" (Acts 8:5), that they "preached good news about the kingdom of God and the name of Jesus Christ" (Acts 8:12). Paul wrote to the Corinthians, "For what we preach is not ourselves, but Jesus Christ as Lord, with ourselves as your servants for Jesus' sake" (2 Cor. 4:5). He, in turn, admonished Timothy to "preach the word" (2 Tim. 4:2), by which he meant the good news concerning salvation through Jesus Christ (2 Tim. 2:8-10). This then is the church's message—not a philosophy, not a system of morality, not finally a form of piety, but Jesus Christ as the Savior and Lord.

1. Jesus Christ Is Savior and Lord of History

As we examine the early Christian proclamation given in Acts and in the Epistles, we sense that in preaching Jesus the apostles were concerned to place Him into the context of human history. C. H. Dodd, after examining methodically the content of preaching in the New Testament, especially in the sermons in Acts and in the Epistles of Paul, has noted that the following elements were stressed:

1) The messianic age, as the age of fulfillment, has dawned.
2) This has taken place through the ministry, death, and resurrection of Jesus.
3) By virtue of His resurrection, Jesus has been exalted to the right hand of God, as messianic head of the New Israel.
4) The Holy Spirit in the church is the sign of Christ's present power and glory.
5) The messianic age will shortly reach its consummation in the return of Christ.

On the basis of these affirmations, there followed an appeal to repent, the offer of forgiveness for sins and of the gift of the Holy Spirit, and the promise of salvation to all who by believing in Jesus Christ would enter the elect community.[5]

While Dodd's attempt to separate preaching and teaching in the New Testament was probably a mistaken effort, his observation that the early church interpreted Christ as Lord of history remains clear. This the church continues to believe and to proclaim: that in the coming of Jesus into the world, God has broken decisively into human history in such a way that Jesus Christ makes an ultimate difference and that we may know by faith that in the end, He will be Lord of all. To say that Jesus is Savior and Lord of history is to acknowledge that all that He has done, is doing, and will yet do has decisive significance. It means, moreover, that we cannot trifle with Jesus Christ, neither with His teachings nor with His person, nor with His claims upon men and on nations. It means also that human history has meaning and that the events of the human story, as they have transpired through the centuries, are not merely chance happenings but in them God is moving toward an ultimate goal for mankind.

In a world where men are overwhelmed with a sense of insignificance and meaninglessness, this is good news. This is gospel.

2. Jesus Christ Is Savior and Lord of Our Lives

A second dimension of the lordship of Christ is the personal relationship which exists between Jesus Christ and His followers. The invitation of Jesus to men to become His followers was and continues to be a personal one. The church proclaims that Jesus is a "personal Savior and Lord." Not only does He confront men in terms of His own personhood, but He also makes a personal claim on our faith, our obedience, our loyalty, and our love. "If any man would come after me, let him deny himself and take up his cross daily and follow me" (Lk. 9:23). "Whoever does not bear his own cross and come after me, cannot be my disciple" (Lk. 14:27). "I am the way, the truth, and the life; no one comes to the Father, but by me'" (Jn. 14:6). "Simon, son of John, do you love me?" (Jn. 21:16).

To those who respond to the call of Christ in obedient faith, He offers forgiveness of sins and a new life which is both abundant and eternal (Jn. 3:3; 10:20, 28). He is, however, the Lord of this new life and not only the Savior of men from their sins. He is not only the Reconciler of those who have been previously alienated, but He becomes Master and Lord of His servants. He is not only One who is to be worshiped, but One who is also to be followed. The frequency of His invitation, "Follow me," becomes the basis for the interpretation of the Christian life as a *Nachfolge Christi* (a following of Christ). This, in turn, means that the whole of life must be subjected to the lordship of Christ, a relationship and a process which calls for rigorous examination of our "thoughts, words, and deeds," all of which are to be brought into subjection to Christ (2 Cor. 10:5; Gal. 3:17).

The authentic Christian message, though it is a message of forgiveness and reconciliation, knows of no proper separation between salvation and discipleship, between faith and obedience, between theology and ethics, or between beliefs and moral standards. The new relationship with Jesus Christ becomes the ground and basis of the new life. The Christian message must include the whole of Jesus Christ making claim upon the whole person.

In these terms, no Christians measure up to the perfect standard. All are "sinners saved by grace," while at the same time they are "saints striving after holiness." In this faith/love encounter with Jesus Christ, we experience both judgment and salvation. The conviction of the early church and ours is that ultimately "there is salvation in no one else, for there is no other name under heaven given among men by which we must be saved" (Acts 4:12).

3. Jesus Christ Is Savior and Lord of the Church and the World Not only is Jesus Lord of history and over His servants individually, He is also Lord over the church and the world. His lordship over the church is sometimes represented by the figure of His headship of the body (Eph. 1:22, 23; 4:15; 5:23; Col. 1:18; 2:10, 19). H. S. Bender notes that this metaphor has at least three meanings, namely, 1) that Christ is the authority over the church, making the church subject to Him through the Holy Spirit, 2) that Christ is the goal of the church, "the total ideal toward which the church directs its efforts" (Eph. 4:15; Col. 2:19), and 3) that Christ and the church are inseparable. If the union with Christ is broken, the body dies.[6]

Eduard Schweizer notes that an additional meaning of Christ's lordship over the church is the idea that "this Lord is stronger than all other powers."[7] In this sense, Christ is not only the One who guides and controls His church by His Spirit, but He is also the one who guards His people as they encounter obstacles, hostility, and enemies while they are seeking to fulfill their life and ministry in the world. While the church is promised no immunity from peril or persecution, it is promised the life-giving, strength-giving presence of the living Christ (Mt. 28:20).

In a somewhat different way, Jesus Christ is also the Lord of the world. He may be, to be sure, the unacknowledged Lord or the unknown Lord, but according to Christian faith, He is nevertheless Lord whether recognized or not. Some of the same passages in Ephesians and Colossians which affirm the lordship of Christ over the church, also affirm His triumph and exaltation over the powers of the world, making Him a cosmic Lord (Eph. 1:21;

Col. 1:15-19; 2:9, 10, 15). This means that ultimately the world cannot escape the meaning of who Christ is and what He is doing in history. Ultimately the kingdom of the world is to become "the kingdom of our Lord and of his Christ, and He shall reign for ever and ever" (Rev. 11:15). This is the great message of Revelation 4 and 5, that Jesus Christ, who is both the Lion of the tribe of Judah and the Lamb that was slain, alone is worthy to open the seal and to be the proper object of universal worship and the Everlasting Sovereign.

This, too, is a part of the Christian message. In fact, it is precisely this lordship of Christ over the whole world which becomes the basis of the Christian witness to the state and to other dimensions of the society beyond the church.[8] It is not only the basis for a prophetic word of doom against the world because of the evil of society, but it is also a basis for the positive social witness of the church. Not only does an unbelieving disobedient society stand in danger of judgment, but it may be assured that Christ, as a cosmic Lord, has good purposes for the universe, that in the end His cause (truth, righteousness, love) must triumph, because He has already triumphed over every form of evil. In fact, the Christian may at times be able to discern that Christ's lordship is manifesting itself in the so-called secular events of the world, though the world itself may have no awareness of the presence of Christ.

The church's message is then on the one hand a very simple gospel: Jesus Christ is Savior and Lord of men. It is, on the other hand, a rich and full gospel—complex, profound, and awe-inspiring in its meaning and implications. It involves the past, the present, and the future of human history. It is both personal and social in its implications. It is both forgiving and demanding. It is "the power of God for salvation to every one who has faith" (Rom. 1:16).

COMMUNICATING THE MESSAGE CLEARLY

The concern about the clarity of the message involves not only a careful definition of the content, but also fidelity in its communication. Just as poor quality mechanical reproduction can ruin for a listener a majestic symphony, so defects in the agents of communication themselves and in their methods may distort and destroy for the world the Christian message.

Christians need to learn from the science of modern communications that the church's message should find expression through a large variety of means and media. We are well aware that in the modern world great advances have been made in the technology of communication. Verbal methods, whether by tongue or pen, represent but one type of communication among many others. Sound, light and darkness, color, varied sequence, surprise, suspense, cartoons, and many varieties of motion are some of the familiar tools with which the modern communicator works.

Christians need not only ask themselves whether they are utilizing, for the communication of the Christian message, the resources which are available, but also whether the use which is made, communicates the Christian message clearly and responsibly. In this the church has much to learn.

Communication by Verbal Means

The proclamation of Jesus Christ by preaching and teaching not only has deep roots in the biblical records, but also has solid validation in Christian history. While we may recognize that these are not the only methods of communicating Christian faith and that, as means, they have their limitation, there is no need to set aside either preaching or teaching in the contemporary church. Preachers and teachers, however, will do well to examine truth which comes from the behavioral sciences concerning how they may make their communication more effective. Reuel Howe in *The Miracle of Dialogue* and other writings is representative of a whole new emphasis calling for better communication between the pulpit and the pew, and between the teacher and his class.[9] Testimony, conversation, discussion, drama, and dialogue are other verbal forms of communicating the Christian message. As we use any one of them we need to ask whether we are employing them most effectively and communicating with greatest clarity.

Communication by Nonverbal Means

The Christian church has much to learn concerning the problems and possibilities of media like music and art. The influence of these media appears to be growing in the contemporary culture and thus becomes of increasing significance to the church.

Included in the more-than-verbal means of communication in the Christian community is the practice of the ordinances which our Lord has taught to His followers. The observance of the Lord's Supper, commemorating His death, bearing witness to the reality of Christian community and anticipating Christ's coming, is in itself a proclamation of the Christian message which involves not only words, but the eating and drinking of the elements and movements of the body in this process.

Baptism on confession of faith, especially as it is practiced in the church of believers is not only a communication of commitment on the part of those who receive baptism, but is likewise a proclamation of the Christian message by the congregation which conducts the service. This, too, has a more-than-verbal character. Where it is practiced, the service of foot washing and the wearing of a prayer veiling are other patterns of behavior which speak their own message without words.

Communication by Witness of the Christian Life

We need not depreciate the significance of words and of nonverbal symbols if we emphasize the need for the dedicated Christian to demonstrate forgiving love, helpful service, and discerning, chaste, and unselfish living. In the ministry of Jesus and in the ministry of the apostolic church, words and deeds were inseparably combined. The question is not whether one should speak or should act, but the question is how to speak and how to act. Apart from the verbal witness, the testimony of a Christian life often remains ambiguous. However, verbal witness without the demonstration of Christian living becomes, to a skeptical world, shallow and empty.

Especially in the light of McLuhan's principle that "the medium is the message," our concern about "clarifying the message" must include also an examination of the medium. In the modern context, the church itself, both in its preaching and in its living is a medium of Christian communication. What is the church saying? By its own being, does it clarify the message or does it cloud it so that Jesus Christ as Savior and Lord is hidden in dense fog?

1 Donald McGavran, "My Dear Friends, My Very Dear Friends," *Church Growth Bulletin,* July 1968, p. 16.

2 This expression was used by John Howard Yoder at an inter-seminary study conference at Bethany Theological Seminary, September 1968.

3 Marshall McLuhan, *Understanding Media: The Extensions of Man* (New York: McGraw-Hill, 1964), pp. 7 ff.

4 Vernon Neufeld, *The Earliest Christian Confessions* (Grand Rapids: Wm. B. Eerdmans, 1964), pp. 141-144.

5 C. H. Dodd, *The Apostolic Preaching* (New York: Harper and Brothers, 1936), pp. 21-23.

6 H. S. Bender, *These Are My People* (Scottdale, Pennsylvania: Herald Press, 1962), pp. 35, 36.

7 Eduard Schweizer, *Lordship and Discipleship* (Naperville, Illinois: Alec R. Allenson, 1960), p. 58. Out of print.

8 John Howard Yoder, *The Christian Witness to the State* (Newton, Kansas: Faith and Life Press, 1964), pp. 8-16.

9 Reuel Howe, *The Miracle of Dialogue* (New York: Seabury Press, 1963).

Chapter 5

The Church in the World

> For God so loved the world that he gave his
> only Son. . . . John 3:16a
> Do not love the world or the things in the
> world. If any one loves the world, love for
> the Father is not in him. 1 John 2:15

The above passages from the Johannine writings placed side by side help to focus the problem faced by the church as it seeks to understand its relationship to the world. On the surface, the passages appear to be in direct conflict, yet we sense that such a conclusion would rest on a misunderstanding of the true meaning of each passage.

Current writings on the church in mission struggle with the question of the relation between church and the world. The weight in the contemporary discussion falls on the side of indicting the church for having separated itself too much from the world, with having become too introverted and obsessed with its own internal needs and affairs, with seeking to maintain its own purity and thus failing to relate meaningfully and redemptively to the world. Such rigorous critiques of the church as Peter Berger's *The Noise of Solemn Assemblies,* Pierre Berton's *The Comfortable Pew,* and J. C. Hoekendijk's *The Church Inside Out* all argue, in different ways, that the church "must get back into the world" if it is to be true to its God-given mission. Failing to do this, these writers would predict that the separated and introverted church is doomed.[1]

The new emphasis on the need for the church to be in the world and involved in its problems is given expression in theological slogans such as "worldly Christianity" or "secular Christianity," which are strange to the ears of most Christians. This is especially true of those who have been taught to avoid worldliness at all costs.

Strange as these expressions may sound to us, it is important that we seek to understand what they mean as we attempt to evaluate what they stand for. It is certainly clear that there is need for deeper probing on the question of the church's relationship to the world.

EXAMINING THE PROBLEM OF CHURCH AND WORLD

One path to a better understanding of the proper relation of church and world is to recognize that the term *world* has a variety of meanings in the New Testament. The English word *world* translates primarily three different Greek words, namely, *oikoumene,* which means "the inhabited earth"; *aion,* which means "eon," "age," or "a period of long duration"; and *kosmos,* which is the most commonly used term.

It is as a translation of the Greek word *kosmos* that *world* has a considerable variety of meanings. C. R. North in *The Interpreter's Dictionary of the Bible*[2] enumerates these as follows:

1. It means the created universe as in Acts 17:24, "The God who made the world and everything in it."

2. It means the earth and/or its inhabitants. In this sense it means either the people of the world, or where they live, or both. This is illustrated in John 1:10, "He was in the world, and the world was made through him, yet the world knew him not."

3. It means "the scene of human activity." In this sense it means the world of human toil, of pain and anxiety, but also of riches and pleasures and all kinds of temporal affairs. It is the world in this sense that we are warned not to love in such a manner that the love of God is displaced (Mt. 16:26; 1 Cor. 7:33, 34; and 1 John 2:15-17).

4. It means "the world at enmity with God." This is the fallen race of mankind in its rebellion. In this sense James 1:27 tells us that true religion is "to keep oneself unstained from the world." James 4:4 asks, "Do you not know that friendship with the world is enmity with God?" So also 2 Peter 1:4 speaks of "the corruption that is in the world" and 2:20 of "the defilements of

the world." The letters of Paul and the Johannine writings frequently use the term *world* in this sense of "sinful mankind." John summarizes in 1 John 5:19 saying, "The whole world is in the power of the evil one."

5. Finally, *kosmos* means "the world Christ came to save." In a sense, this is the same world of fallen mankind spoken of above, but seen from the perspective of God's purpose in Christ. Here John 3:16, "God so loved the world," and 2 Corinthians 5:19, "God was in Christ reconciling the world to himself" are typical and familiar passages.

Having reviewed the biblical uses of the term *world*, we need also to be aware that in English we employ still additional meanings which are suggested in such common expressions as "in this world and the next," "the academic world," "the animal world," "it makes a world of difference," "what in the world?" or "it is simply out of this world!"

When we then discuss the topic of church and world, or when we try to discover what is meant by "worldly Christianity," we must be sure that we understand exactly what each person means by the terms that he is using. No Christian considers the world totally evil when he is speaking of it in the sense of the created universe. Neither does he hold that men are as bad as they can possibly be when he speaks of the world as sinful mankind. However, to speak of the world without any clarification as to what one means or to ignore completely the biblical understanding of the sinfulness of man is to introduce meanings which are confusing and even theologically irresponsible. The new emphasis on John 3:16 as a theological basis for identification with the world tends to place the emphasis on the part which says, "God so loved the world." At times such discussion fails to recognize properly that the same passage implies a "perishing world" which is the essential concern of God's love in sending Jesus Christ into the world. Along with a new appreciation of God's love for the world, we need also a new awareness of the predicament of this world and the reasons for this, as well as the provision God has made in Christ for the redemption and reconciliation of the world.

A passage which helps to bring the question of church and world into biblical focus is John 17. Here Jesus speaks of His own mission to the world and then prays for His disciples and for those who would come to believe in Him through their mission to the world. He speaks of "the world" in the very broad sense of "the created universe" (vv. 5 and 25), but He also speaks of how His disciples have been given to Him out of the world (v. 6) and of how the world has hated the disciples "because they are not of the world, even as I am not of the world" (v. 14). He implies the lostness of the world apart from His own coming (vv. 3-5), but also implies the redeemability of the world (vv. 21, 23). Though He speaks of praying directly for His disciples and for the church, not for the world (v. 9), yet essentially it is the salvation of the world which is His deep concern. His own mission and the mission of the disciples have precisely the purpose of bringing His salvation to this world.

Here then we have placed side by side three expressions which may help to give us a formula for a proper understanding of the relationship of church and world. These are:

"In the world" (v. 11),

"Not of the world, even as I am not of the world" (vv. 14, 16),

"As thou didst send me into the world, so I have sent them into the world" (v. 18).

In the past, the tendency has been to focus on the expressions "in the world," and "but not of the world." In various communities and at various times in the history of God's people, the emphasis has fallen on one or the other of these expressions. To isolate either expression and to ignore the other leads to distortion. Those who emphasize the importance of being "in the world" tend to lose the truth of nonconformity. On the other hand, those who emphasize the phrase "not of the world," tend to remove themselves so far from sinful men, either literally by withdrawing into closed communities, or spiritually by living on a high pillar of personal piety that they have real difficulty in fulfilling their mission to the world.

The best answer to the problem of church and world comes

when we focus our attention on the fact that we have been sent into the world even as Christ was sent into the world. By keeping in the foreground the person and the mission of Jesus Christ and His mandate to the church to be His ambassador of reconciliation in the world (2 Cor. 5:20), we have a formula which can help us through the dilemmas of the relationship to the world. Jesus Christ becomes for us both pattern and power for this relationship. To walk with Him is to walk in the world as He walked. This means identification with men in their plight, but not in their sin. To walk with Him is also to remain completely humble and inoffensive in our piety. To be in the world, as Christ was, is to love sinful men with the same compassion that took Him to the cross.

The Church's Responsibility in Society

The basic concern of this lesson is to help us understand the need for the church to be "in the world" and to discern and discharge its responsibility to society.

In one sense the church is in the world as a "given" and is not something to be argued about. Even as Jesus was literally "in the world," as One who mingled in the society of men, was subject to social pressures, needed to relate to government officials (Pilate and Herod), confronted the poor and underprivileged, as well as the outcasts of society, whether these were rich like Zacchaeus or poor like blind Bartimaeus, even so the church has been throughout history and is today "in the world."

The fact that the church is also a human institution and not only divine, links it with the rest of society in an inescapable solidarity. Wherever the church has come into being, it has found it necessary to identify in some ways with its larger cultural setting. Since not all aspects of humanness are necessarily sinful, the church is not to be criticized for those aspects of its humanness which are not contrary to God's will or to the Spirit of Christ. In fact, it is precisely the humanness of the church which becomes the bridge to the rest of human society, the point of contact which can make possible the ministry of reconciliation.

The call to the church, however, in this matter is not to become simply more human and less Christian, as some have suggested. The call is rather to understand Jesus Christ better in terms of His humanity and then to be more like Him. Growth in this direction would at the same time be growth toward becoming more Christian and more human.

Beyond the call to recognize its humanness and its solidarity with the rest of society, the call of God to the church in the discharge of its responsibility to society is at least threefold.

Evangelism

The first call is to evangelism. Jesus gave the Great Commission to His disciples, "Go therefore and make disciples of all nations, baptizing them in the name of the Father and of the Son and of the Holy Spirit, teaching them to observe all that I have commanded you; and lo, I am with you always, to the close of the age" (Mt. 28:19, 20). This Great Commission was recognized by the Anabaptists as being binding on the entire people of God, not only on its appointed leaders or its missionaries. The task of "making disciples" includes the preaching ministry, but does not stop with it. What Jesus calls for is a full-orbed incorporation of new believers into comprehending and obedient discipleship. This will call for the utilization of many tools and various means. When the churches cease to be agents of evangelism in the midst of a society which is either ignorantly or intelligently non-Christian, they fail to discharge their responsibility to that society from the perspective of the New Testament.

Love in Action

A second mandate to the church is to respond to human need in active love even as Jesus Christ Himself did. "Give ye them to eat" (Mk. 6:37) was the command of Jesus to the Twelve when the five thousand had gathered and were hungry. The parable of the Good Samaritan and the description of the last judgment (Mt. 25) are powerful appeals to active social ministries of love to the hurt, the dispossessed, the oppressed, and the many other "forgotten people" of a society. Scarcely any word is stronger than 1 John 3:17, 18, "If any one has the world's goods and sees his brother in need, yet closes his heart against him, how does God's love abide in him? Little children, let us not love in word or speech but in deed and in truth."

This dimension of the ministry of reconciliation has made its strong appeal to congregations of the Anabaptist-Mennonite heritage, resulting in large and dynamic programs of relief and rehabilitation, disaster ministries, educational ministries abroad and in the homeland, mental health services, and ministries to the offender. Not only have congregations given relatively generous financial support to such programs, but many persons of various ages have become personally involved in such ministries in a wide variety of settings, sometimes on a short-range but also frequently on a long-range basis. The call to feed the hungry, to bind up the wounds of society, and to rehabilitate those who have been struck down by the misfortunes of life is essentially a call to translate love into Christian social action.

Prophetic Witness

There is a third dimension of God's call to His people which has not always been seen as clearly as the mandate to evangelize and the imperative to minister in love where there is real human need. This is the call to give a prophetic witness in society.

This call also has its deep biblical roots. These roots are profuse in the Old Testament where prophets rose up in response to the call of God and declared to their political rulers and to the people of the nations "the direction in which God was moving in their day." Amos, Micah, Jeremiah, and Isaiah are all notable and familiar examples of prophets who made pronouncements on both social and political issues of the time.

In the New Testament, as John Howard Yoder has pointed out, Christ's own encounters with society, His teaching, as well as His lordship over "church and world," all have social and political implications which become the basis of "the Christian witness to the State."[3]

The Christian's prophetic witness to society, however, not only involves political structures (nation, city council) but also the economic structures (business, management, and labor), educational structures (the university, the local school), and the structures of mass communication (television, journalism). In fact, whatever social structures may arise to become powers of the world may come into conflict with the realization of the kingdom of God. These become the deep concerns of prophetic Christian witness.

Christian witness in this area is being probed with great diligence in the contemporary church. Study conferences have been held on church and society on denominational, national, and world levels. While there is a considerable divergence of conviction concerning the particular ways in which the prophetic witness of the church is to be brought to bear on the structures of society, there is growing unanimity that this witness is a part of the church's total responsibility. As Elmer Neufeld puts it, "When we are thoroughly motivated by the love of the Christ of the cross—when we all actually take our neighbor's interests as seriously as our own, our concerns will appropriately find an expression in actions that do have political relevance."[4]

SOME CONTEMPORARY SOCIAL ISSUES

It is impossible to deal with all the kinds of issues which arise as the church considers its prophetic responsibility in contemporary society. Only a few such issues are introduced for illustrative purposes to suggest still other questions which need to be faced. Some of the issues most commonly discussed at present are 1) war and peace, 2) racial justice, 3) the alleviation of poverty, 4) the church's response to the "population explosion," and 5) the church's role in "revolution." The issue of whether violence is ever justified in bringing about social and political change is a live contemporary topic.

1. What are the most appropriate and effective ways for the church to witness in the area of political concern?

Mennonites have generally agreed that they ought not to participate in the military functions of the state, believing that war is contrary to the will of God. They have sought and have been granted alternative patterns of service in view of being conscientious objectors to war. This has been a prophetic witness with political implications. During the Vietnam war, however, a broad resistance to military service has developed, especially among students in the United States, not so much on religious as on pragmatic grounds. The objections to the Vietnam war have been expressed in dramatic and sometimes bizarre ways, such as burning draft cards, blocking out recruiters for military service on campuses, as well as those recruiting students for chemical research leading to the production of war materials. In one case, at least, a conscientious objector to war set fire to his own person and destroyed himself. These dramatic methods of protest raise the question whether the Mennonite witness to the state in this matter goes far enough, or whether new patterns should be found. Is the pattern of alternative service still the most effective way of witnessing in this area? If so, which forms of alternative service are most effective and under what conditions?

2. What is the significance of Christians exercising their right to vote?

At one time a conviction prevailed that nonresistant Mennonites should not exercise the franchise. It was considered inconsistent for a person to refuse military service on the one hand, yet vote for political offices, or possibly even run for political office himself. Gradually this position has changed with Mennonites beginning to vote at local levels, and later on at national levels on such issues as prohibition. It is probable that by this time, the majority of Mennonites exercise the right to vote though often with considerable misgivings as to the significance of this action. In some congregations, however, issues in national elections have seemed very significant. In one case a congregation all but reached a complete consensus on endorsing a particular candidate for the presidency. Not long after his election, however, he led the nation directly into war and developed policies which were quite in contradiction to the convictions of the same Mennonite congregation which virtually endorsed him. Since the alternatives in national elections are scarcely ever a choice between completely good and completely bad candidates, is not the exercise of political franchise in the present situation an exercise in compromise?

This may raise again the question as to whether the church's responsibility in the area of political concern may not rest at a substantially higher level than a preoccupation with the question of political activity. However, to leave the questions of political activity in the hands of others may indeed be a form of Christian irresponsibility. The answers in this area do not come easily.

3. To what extent is it the church's responsibility to invest some of its financial resources in social programs?

Generally, Christians, including Mennonites, have been encouraged to support certain kinds of proposed legislation such as civil rights measures or provisions for the alleviation of poverty by writing letters to their congressmen. In some cases Christians have also been participating in marches and demonstrations intending to dramatize the significance of such legislation. A somewhat more recent form of response has been for denominational bodies to invest substantial percentages of their own financial resources in social programs, such as, "the war against poverty."

This raises the question as to where the church's funds should be invested. For the church to invest its funds directly in the alleviation of poverty, though this might seem to be but a drop in the bucket, would have the witness value of demonstrating that the church means business in this area. It also makes it possible to carry on certain programs apart from any political involvements whatsoever. On the other hand, it must be recognized that funds invested in poverty alleviation cannot then also be used for educational and evangelistic purposes or even for ministries of reconciliation in other areas. Moreover, it is generally recognized that the lot of the poor in America is better than that of vast proportions of the world's population. How much of the church's resources should then be expended to help the American poor? This raises the question, What is poverty? And how are the poor helped most? Does Acts 3 have relevance here?

4. Guy F. Hershberger, frequently in his writings, calls the church the "conscience of society."[5] This calls for ethical witness in matters in which society fails to serve its own best interests corporately and the best interests of individual persons. In the past, the church has witnessed against slavery and more recently against racial discrimination. Much more is being done and remains to be done in this area.

Does not the church, however, also have a major responsibility to witness to the power structures of business and industry?

In recent years there have developed a number of industrial missions in Europe and in North America. The Detroit Industrial Mission is one of the pioneers and among the best known. Here an attempt is made to witness to economic structures particularly as it is observed that injustice prevails at some point. Industrial missions vary in their objectives, but the focus seems to be on witness to structures rather than witnessing to individual persons. Should the church become more involved in witness of this kind? And, if so, what are some of the pitfalls which we should avoid?

5. This also leads us to questions concerning the church's responsibility toward power structures in the area of mass communications and in the entertainment world. That these structures are not generally motivated by Christian concerns, but primarily by a profit motive is broadly recognized. Among the results is the profusion of violence and sex in television and of the spectacular and sensual in many books and magazines. How can the church respond in a significant way in this area?

6. At one time Mennonites were much concerned about the issue of alcoholism and tended to take the side of prohibition in responding to this problem. National prohibition did not solve the problem of alcoholism. Meanwhile, the problem has become much more widespread, yet Mennonites along with other Christian groups seem to have less and less to say about it. Is the silence of Christians in this area a part of social irresponsibility?

7. The debates over "the new morality" in the area of sex ethics, together with the discussions in the Roman Catholic Church on the issue of birth control, have focused considerable attention on the contemporary attitude toward sex and sexuality. It is generally agreed that in society at large there is a reaction against the older so-called Puritanical standards, and an increase in freedom in sex behavior. Does the church have a greater responsibility in this area than it has recognized in the past? If so, how can it deal more effectively with issues which are as intimate and personal as questions of sex ethics? Is it possible to develop guidelines which will be accepted by Christian young people and their parents as well as by the community as a whole in these matters?

1 Peter Berger, *The Noise of Solemn Assemblies* (Garden City: Doubleday, 1961); Pierre Berton, *The Comfortable Pew* (Philadelphia: Lippincott, 1965); J. C. Hoekendijk, *The Church Inside Out* (Philadelphia: Westminster Press, 1966).

2 *The Interpreter's Dictionary of the Bible* (New York: Abingdon, 1962), Vol. 4, pp. 876-888.

3 John Howard Yoder, *The Christian Witness to the State* (Newton, Kansas: Faith and Life Press, 1964).

4 Elmer Neufeld, "Christian Responsibility in the Political Situation," *Mennonite Quarterly Review,* April 1958, p. 161.

5 Guy F. Hershberger, *The Way of the Cross in Human Relations* (Scottdale, Pennsylvania: Herald Press, 1958), p. 43, *et al.*

Chapter 6

The Church Not of the World

In the current discussions on the need for the church to become involved in the world and relevant to its deep needs, very little attention is being given to the clear biblical teaching that the church is not of this world. In part, this omission may be a reaction against earlier emphases in Puritan, Pietist, and also Anabaptist circles which emphasized too much the church's separation from the world. In part, the omission appears to be an oversight or a neglect of another dimension of biblical teaching. The tendency to swing like a pendulum is understandable, yet its results may also be very tragic. The overlooking of a significant segment of biblical truth is never justified.

Christians of the Anabaptist-Mennonite heritage, along with Brethren and Friends, have an unusually rich background to confront the issues of the separation of church and world, sometimes called "nonconformity" or simply "dissent."[1] While not all of the history of nonconformity in these groups is a credit to them, and while it is precisely various interpretations of nonconformity and the attempts to apply these to contemporary issues which have resulted in legalism and have led to numerous schisms, divisions, and even migrations among these groups, there are strong positive elements in this background which ought not to be lost in the current emphasis on mission and involvement.

Among the significant writings on the meaning of nonconformity in the twentieth century, is J. C. Wenger's *Separated Unto God*.[2] Not only does this book set forth profusely and in an orderly way the biblical basis for nonconformity, but it seeks to apply biblical guidelines to numerous practical problems of the separated life, including the Christian's speech, his recreational and cultural life, his marriage and family life, questions of organizational memberships and relationships, simplicity in worship, stewardship and mutual aid in the Christian brotherhood, the Christian's relation to the state, and his relationship to the industrial world. While no attempt is made to give precise and detailed answers on all these questions, the issues are illuminated in the light of biblical teaching, which is as far as this kind of treatment can go.

Two observations are of special importance as we continue this study. The first is recognized in J. C. Wenger's book title, *Separated Unto God.* This title, carefully chosen, accents the positive meaning of nonconformity. While negative statements of nonconformity are biblical and legitimate, there is a danger that these, if overemphasized, cause this dimension of truth to be seen in a negativistic way. In part, it is precisely this negative image which has prompted silence on the subject or has led to a reaction against it. While "separation" is the basic concept to be dealt with, it is important to note *to what* or *to whom* the people of God are to be separated and why this is important to them in the fulfillment of their mission in the world. It is only a secondary concern to note what they have been separated *from,* though realistically the positive and the negative dimensions of separation must be seen in relationship to each other.

A second significant observation is that the principle of separation of church and world is not simply a Mennonite tradition. It is a basic principle which belongs to all the "free churches." The eminent Cambridge scholar, Peter T. Forsyth, delivered six lectures on "The Spiritual Principle of Nonconformity," which were published in 1896 under the general title, *The Charter of the Church.*[3] The basic thesis of his lectures was that the true church is a "free church" as over against an "established church." In the context of the time, the established church identified church and state (world) much too closely and thus put the gospel and its implications in jeopardy. Nonconformity, then, in its historical meaning, has not been simply a question of whether one may have radio or television in the home. It is a question of whether the church is indeed free to obey its living Lord as over against being under the power of the state or of other powers.

Having recognized the strong and clear biblical call to the church to be involved in mission in the world, it is important now to recognize also the call to separation from the world. The call to Abraham, which was in principle a call to mission, is at the same time a call to separation. "Go from your country and your kindred and your father's house to the land that I will show you" (Gen. 12:1). The Book of Hebrews reports, "By faith Abraham obeyed when he was called to go out to a place which he was to receive as an inheritance; and he went out, not knowing where he was to go. By faith he sojourned in the land of promise, as in a foreign land, living in tents with Isaac and Jacob, heirs with him of the same promise. For he looked forward to the city which has foundations, whose builder and maker is God" (Heb. 11:8-10).

In this call to Abraham and his response to it, we see the beginning of a people which was to be separate from the other nations of the world because of a unique mission. The mission was to have a universal significance but its implementation was to come about through a particular people. This was the people of the covenant whom God had "chosen" to be His servant people in the world. The separateness of this people was a part of its servanthood in the world.

Through Moses God said to the people of Israel, "I am the Lord your God, who have separated you from the peoples. . . . You shall be holy to me; for I the Lord am holy, and have separated you from the peoples, that you should be mine" (Lev. 20:24, 26).

Under the Old Covenant, this call to separation came to have a variety of applications involving many aspects of Israel's living. It included various moral and ceremonial laws as these are recorded in Exodus, Leviticus, and Deuteronomy; some economic regulations (such as tithing, the Year of Jubilee, special provision for the poor, the prohibition of taking interest); particular worship patterns and sacrifices; as well as regulations concerning foods, clothing, and agricultural practices.

Central to all of these regulations was the notion that Israel was to be "a holy nation, belonging to Jehovah, dedicated to holiness of life, to faith and obedience, and called to exhibit the character of God here on earth."[4]

The New Testament lifts the Old Testament principle of separation to a new level and makes it applicable to the Christian church. Probably the most familiar New Testament injunction to separation is Romans 12:1, 2:

> I appeal to you therefore, brethren, by the mercies of God, to present your bodies as a living sacrifice, holy and acceptable to God, which is your spiritual worship. Do not be conformed to this world but be transformed by the renewal of your mind, that you may prove what is the will of God, what is good and acceptable and perfect.

J. B. Phillips has rendered the second verse in an arresting and pungent way as follows:

> Don't let the world around you squeeze you into its own mold, but let God remold your minds from within, so that you may prove in practice that the plan of God for you is good, meets all his demands, and moves toward the goal of true maturity.

In 2 Corinthians 6:14—7:1 is found Paul's most elaborate appeal to separation:

> Do not be mismated with unbelievers. For what partnership have righteousness and iniquity? Or what fellowship has light with darkness? What accord has Christ with Belial? Or what has a believer in common with an unbeliever? What agreement has the temple of God with idols? For we are the temple of the living God; as God said,
>
> "I will live in them and move among them,
>> and I will be their God,
>> and they shall be my people.
> Therefore come out from them,
>> and be separate from them, says the Lord,
>> and touch nothing unclean;
> then I will welcome you,
>> and I will be a father to you,
>> and you shall be my sons and daughters,
> says the Lord Almighty."
>
> Since we have these promises, beloved, let us cleanse ourselves from every defilement of body and spirit, and make holiness perfect in the fear of God.

In this passage Paul is enjoining the Christians of Corinth, living in the midst of a society with less than Christian standards, to maintain conduct which distinguishes them from those who are not of the fellowship of believers. Clearly there is implied a difference between *church* and *world*. The basis for the appeal leads Paul back into the Old Testament where God calls on His people to maintain their identity in order that they may fulfill His holy purposes in the world.

However, not only Paul, but also John calls for separation from the world and the things in the world, in such a passage as 1 John 2:15, 16:

> Do not love the world or the things in the world. If any one loves the world, love for the Father is not in him. For all that is in the world, the lust of the flesh and the lust of the eyes and the pride of life, is not of the Father but is of the world. And the world passes away, and the lust of it; but he who does the will of God abides for ever.

Likewise, Peter in writing to the scattered Christian communities in Asia Minor, seeing Christian faith and life under the image of a pilgrimage, writes:

> Beloved, I beseech you as aliens and exiles to abstain from the passions of the flesh that wage war against your soul. Maintain good conduct among the Gentiles, so that in case they speak against you as wrongdoers, they may see your good deeds and glorify God on the day of visitation. 1 Peter 2:11, 12

The biblical call to the separation of church and world, then, does not rest on a few isolated proof texts, but is embedded deeply in large biblical themes and concepts which run through both the Old and the New Testaments. Basic is the notion that God's people are to be a "holy people" set apart for purposes of obedience and service from any patterns of life in the world which would interfere with their ministry or would weaken it in any way.

Moreover, there is the concept of the people of God being "pilgrims and strangers" on the earth, with "no abiding city here" but with a "citizenship in heaven."[5] This implies that from the perspective of the Christian, all of the values and claims of this world are relative and can never be absolute. This calls for a kind of detachment from the world on the part of the people of God.

BASIC CONCERNS IN SEPARATION

While the interpretation of separation of church and world and its application to particular issues in life have varied through Christian history and will continue to do so, let us now identify three basic concerns which arise out of the conviction that the church "is not of the world."

The Purity of the Church

The first concern is for the purity of the church. Under the Old Covenant, God was concerned about the purity of Israel. In the New Testament, Paul in writing to the Ephesians, speaks of the love of Christ for the church, His sacrifice on behalf of the church, and His purpose to set apart the church as a cleansed body, to be presented before Him "in splendor, without spot or wrinkle or any such thing, that she might be holy and without blemish" (Eph. 5:25-27).

Sometimes it is forgotten that this passage is part of a section whose basic concern is to enjoin husbands to love their wives. The love of Christ for the church is used as pattern and motivation for proper love in the marriage relationship. However, the ideal of the pure church does come to expression here. More often, it is forgotten that the ideal of purity here is seen eschatologically, that is, "as it will be in the end."

Two perils emerge as Christians seek to respond to this concern for the purity of the church. The one is that purity is conceived in moralistic terms and its achievement is then undertaken through legalistic methods. To conceive of the purity of the church in this way is to overlook the much deeper dimensions of God's working and man's response in the life of the church. Moreover, to attempt to actualize the pure church through external legalistic measures simply will not work. Ecclesiastical legislation has never achieved the kind of purity that the New Testament talks about.

70

The other danger is the abandonment of the concern for the pure church since we do not see it anywhere. This abandonment may take the form of an attempt to start still another new fellowship which will at least be more faithful than all the other current efforts. It may, on the other hand, lead to a passive acceptance of the unfaithfulness which is currently to be found in the churches. Or, it may conceivably lead to complete despair with the church and a retreat into individualistic Christianity, or perchance the abandonment of Christian faith itself.

This, in principle, is the error of perfectionism which tends to insist on 100 percent or nothing. It is based on the failure to discern that the church is both human and divine, that it is continuously involved in a process of struggle and growth, that it is at one and the same time the fellowship of "sinners saved by grace" and "saints striving after holiness." It is a point of view which cannot live with paradoxical elements which make up the actual life of the church, whether in the New Testament or in contemporary expression. None of the congregations described in the New Testament records was pure in an absolutely perfect sense. Certainly, the congregations in Corinth, in Philippi, and in Thessalonica had their failures, yet Paul recognized them as true expressions of the church of God and called them "saints."

The purification of the church ultimately is the work of God among His people. Only the Holy Spirit can renew the church and cleanse it from all its faults. However, the concern for the purity of the church also implies a divine discontent with things as they are, an openness on the part of God's people to the renewing and cleansing work of His Spirit, and a willingness to obey new light as it comes.

The Discerning Church

A second basic concern is for discernment. The church which is not of the world is called to be a discerning fellowship. It follows from the call to separation of church and world that individual Christians and the congregations of which they are a part must continuously evaluate and reevaluate the standards and practices of the world society of which they are a part, as well as their own behavior as a people of God. These practices are examined in the light of God's will as it is known through the Scriptures and illumined by the Holy Spirit.

In writing to the Philippians, after Paul had expressed his gratitude for them and for their fellowship, he says, "And it is my prayer that your love may abound more and more, with knowledge and all discernment, so that you may approve what is excellent, and may be pure and blameless for the day of Christ, filled with the fruits of righteousness which come through Jesus Christ, to the glory and praise of God" (Phil. 1:9-11). While Christians are warned against becoming faultfinding and condemning persons, they are strongly enjoined to become discerning and discriminating persons, able to make distinctions not only between right and wrong but also "that they may approve what is excellent." Sometimes the critical choices in life are between what men call good and what may, in fact, be "the excellent" or "the best way."

The function of discernment is to be viewed with such seriousness that it cannot be left to the individual believer alone to make his own judgments. To be sure, in many of the details of life, decisions are of a private or familistic character. However, discernment is to become a function of the local congregation. The fellowship of believers gathering around the open Scriptures, led by the Holy Spirit in the presence of the living Christ, the head of the church, is to search diligently for "the wisdom that is from above" in deciding how to live and serve in the midst of the world.

To speak of the world as writing the agenda for the church tends to confuse the issue. While it is quite true that what is going on in the world must help to shape what the church talks about, the control of the agenda ought to be, theologically speaking, the jurisdiction of the Holy Spirit. The Christian community stands constantly between the Word and the world. The Holy Spirit, who is ultimately the author of the Word and who is working in the world, is alone qualified to determine the agenda.

The Disciplined Church

A third basic concern of the church which is not of the world is discipline.

While church discipline has admittedly often been abused, has sometimes been rigid and unredemptive in spirit, and ineffective in reclaiming the offender in its results, it too represents a biblical concern which may not be abandoned. The New Testament church was concerned with both personal and corporate church discipline. Its basic purpose and approach are outlined in Matthew 18, especially verses 15-35. It is significant to sense how strong the emphasis on forgiveness is in this passage.

In reevaluating the place of discipline in the church today, the educative rather than the punitive approach must be stressed. Personal and group counseling in the context of a concerned congregation are probably far more effective means of church discipline in reclaiming persons than some of the more formal methods of admonition and excommunication which have been used in the past. This is not to say that excommunication is never called for. The New Testament makes room for it.

What must be clear in this lesson, however, is that the separated church is also a disciplined church. It is of real significance that many of the renewal movements in contemporary Christianity are again emphasizing the place of discipline in the life of the congregation. Those who become members of renewal groups must commit themselves to explicit disciplines and their failure to abide by these calls for counsel, reconciliation, and restoration in order that the life of the disciplined group may be carried forward.

IMPLICATIONS

When Jesus called men to discipleship, He admonished them to "count the cost." When a church seeks to be faithful both in mission and in separation, this too has costly implications and consequences.

One Implication Is Tension

To take God's call to be in but not of the world seriously, places the church in a position of being pulled in two directions at the same time. On the one side, the church is pulled toward Christ, constantly seeking to be faithful to Him in truth and love. On the other side, the church is constantly pulled toward the world, for if one truly loves the world in a Christian sense, one is drawn toward it, one agonizes with its failures, its hurts, its false ambitions, its sin and the consequences. Moreover, because the church is also human, the pull toward the world does not arise only out of empathy. In part, this pull is temptation to become like the world.

This tension of standing between Chirst and the world can be creative and challenging or it may become distracting and destructive. It becomes destructive when it undermines the integrity of the church, when it leads to compromise, and when it clouds the witness of the church before the world. This happens whenever the church fails to listen carefully to the Holy Spirit about its style of life, its patterns of private and public worship, its relationships, and its attitude and behavior patterns.

To be faithful, the church ought not seek to escape this tension. The tension is escaped illegitimately when the church moves too far either in the direction of avoiding mission in the world, or in the direction of ignoring the call to be separate from the world. Some Christians are entirely too comfortable in the church, ignoring their responsibility in mission. They enjoy their prayers, their Bible studies, their hymns, their sacraments, and their fellowship dinners, but have neither time nor energy nor disposition to give themselves in ministry to people outside of the church who are in deep human need. Thus, they escape the tension, but they fail in mission.

Other Christians are entirely too comfortable in the world, having "made peace" with it rather than with God. They have adopted the behavior patterns of non-Christians and reflect the world's perspectives, judgments, and values. Though at one time they may have begun their identification with the world in an effort to help the world, they have, in fact, themselves been conquered by the world. Instead of overcoming the world by faith (1 Jn. 5:4), they have been overcome by the world.

A Second Implication Is Suffering

This should not come as a surprise. Even in the Old Testament, the servant of the Lord is portrayed as a suffering servant (Is. 53). Jesus was the suffering servant par excellence both in His early ministry and in His death on the cross; He calls men to walk with Him in the way of the cross, that is, the way of suffering servant-hood.

It is precisely at this point that the servant is not greater than his Lord (Jn. 15:20). Jesus suffered, on the one hand, because of His sensitive awareness of men's burdens and sins. He suffered, on the other hand, because of the world's hostility to Him as He remained faithful to truth. Though He came to be the reconciler, to break down the hostilities which separated men, He could do this only by absorbing the hostility which was focused upon Him.

In a similar manner the church suffers if it is in the world because it becomes sensitive to the depth of the problems and pain of the world in its predicament. The Christian identifies with the world so closely that the world's pain becomes his pain. Unfair as it may appear, the church identifies with the corporate sins of its society and recognizes and confesses a common guilt.

The church not being of the world, comes to be hated by the world (Jn. 16:19). The church is a witness to truth and thus cannot condone pretense and falsehood. It is dedicated to universal good and, therefore, must take its stand against the large variety of forms of selfishness which the world sets up. The church is dedicated to speak what it knows rather than to remain silent. For these and other reasons the church comes to be the object of the world's hostility. "Woe to you, when all men speak well of you" (Lk. 6:26). When the world has become so comfortable with the church that all traces of hostility have vanished, "the salt" apparently has lost its tang. Then, according to the judgment of Jesus, "it is good for nothing."

A Third Consequence Is Strength

If the church in faithfulness continues to live in tension, faces and absorbs the suffering which comes because of faithfulness to Christ, a third consequence is strength. The church in tension, ready to suffer, is already a church of strength and is promised the strengthening presence of the living Christ. "Finally, be strong in the Lord and in the strength of his might" (Eph. 6:10). "I can do all things in him who strengthens me" (Phil. 4:13).

Facing tension and resistance helps the church to become strong because it must rely on the Lord for help. The church is kept alert, and must maintain the disciplines of discerning Bible study and prayer. The church must live by faith.

The strength of the suffering church lies in the fact that witness does not come in the form of success. It comes rather in what the Christian is individually, and what the church is corporately. The witness of the suffering church comes in the form of courageous faithfulness.

The history of God's people indicates that tension and suffering have contributed far more to the vitality and effectiveness of the church's witness than numerical, material, or psychological successes. The call to be involved in both mission and separateness is not a call to ease but it is the way to glory.

1 John Howard Yoder, "The Prophetic Dissent of Anabaptism," in Guy F. Hershberger, ed., *The Recovery of the Anabaptist Vision* (Scottdale, Pennsylvania: Herald Press, 1957), pp. 93-104.

2 J. C. Wenger, *Separated Unto God* (Scottdale, Pennsylvania: Herald Press, 1951).

3 P. T. Forsyth, *The Charter of the Church* (London, Alexander, and Shepherd, 1896).

4 Wenger, *op. cit.*, p. 17.

5 H. S. Bender, "Nonconformity," *Mennonite Encyclopedia* (Scottdale, Pennsylvania: Mennonite Publishing House, 1955), Vol. III, p. 891.

Chapter 7

The Church Gathered

In her penetrating book, *Journey Inward, Journey Outward,* Elizabeth O'Connor affirms the bipolar need for the church to *gather* for worship and nurture and then to *scatter* for witness and service. In the preface she reports the following observation concerning the contemporary controversy over the relative importance of the gathering of the church for its own meetings and the scattering of the church in mission. She says:

> Those congregations whose stress has been on the inward— worship, small prayer meetings, and study programs—are sensing that the call to wholeness involves more than this, while those who have abandoned this part of the inward journey to carve out in the cities the new forms of the church are receiving hints that all is not well with these missions.[1]

Elton Trueblood, in *The Incendiary Fellowship,* makes essentially the same point when in his discussion of the church's ministry in the world, he uses the analogy of "the base" and "the field." Both of these elements are necessary for a successful operation. Every ministry must have a base. There needs to be a gathered congregation which becomes the base for the ministry. However, there must also be a "field" where the congregation's ministry finds expression. Jesus Himself said, "The field is the world" (Mt. 13: 38).

Trueblood summarizes:

> "The only hope for the renewal of the church lies in the recognition of its essential polarity. The church must exist *in* the world, but, paradoxically, it must exist, at the same time, *apart from* the world. . . . We are making a great forward step when we realize that there is no inevitable contradiction between the idea of the scattered church and the idea of the gathered church. We gather in order to scatter!"[2]

Having recognized in the previous two lessons the need for

the church to be both in the world but not of the world, in this chapter and the next we observe the double imperatives of the gathering and the scattering of the church, and the necessity of seeing these two dimensions of the life and ministry of the church in their proper relationship to each other.

Those who have been critical of the validity and adequacy of the church's patterns for gathering in the past, have rendered a service to the church by forcing it to ask again, Why gather? Not only are young people in Christian homes asking this. Inevitably it is asked by those who face the questions of supporting financially local church programs, of arranging their busy schedules so as to make possible attendance at church gatherings, as well as by those who are responsible for the arrangement of the gatherings. The question needs to be asked whether one thinks of the meeting of a small group fellowship, a local congregation, or a conference fellowship, whether at regional, national, or even world levels. The substantial investment which the church has made and continues to make in its own gathering requires both examination and justification.

WHY THE CHURCH GATHERS

"For where two or three are gathered in my name, there am I in the midst of them" (Mt. 18:20). This alone, understood with all of its implications, would give Christians adequate ground for continuing to come together. The gathering of the early disciples was occasioned by the desire to be in the presence of Jesus in order that they might learn of Him and serve Him. The assembling of the early Christians "on the first day of the week" was sustained and regularized by their experience of His living presence in their midst as they met in His Name. They continued to pray for His full and final coming as is expressed by the prayer *Maranatha* (Come, Lord Jesus), apparently commonly voiced in the early church.

After the dramatic event on the Day of Pentecost, we read that the early Christians "devoted themselves to the apostles' teaching and fellowship, to the breaking of bread and the prayers" (Acts

2:42). "And day by day, attending the temple together and breaking bread in their homes, they partook of food with glad and generous hearts, praising God and having favor with all the people" (Acts 2:46).

The Church Gathers for Worship

We have already recognized the importance of worship in the life of the early church. Eduard Schweizer notes that in the New Testament, "It is . . . essential for the service (meeting for worship) and for the church order that it expresses, that the church is actually physically together."[3] He notes that in early Christian worship, the preaching of the Word had a decisive and central place, that the Lord's Supper played a large role, and that the worship order itself, with its hymns, Scriptures, and prayers included both "free" and "fixed" forms. There was freedom in the sense of flexibility and the possibility that if some member of the gathered assembly had a word for the congregation, he would have opportunity to share it with the others (1 Cor. 14), but there were also regular patterns which gave structure and continuity to the worship services.

Christian denominations differ considerably in the patterns of worship which have been developed. In some groups the fixed forms have predominated, whereas in other groups the emphasis is on freedom. Currently, many groups have begun to reevaluate worship patterns and to experiment with new patterns, or at least to vary what was formerly considered a fixed order. Responses to the changes taking place have been varied. It would not seem unreasonable that with all of the changes taking place in other dimensions of life in the contemporary world, that meaningful changes in worship patterns can be found. On the other hand, worship is vastly more than experimentation. Congregations which try out new patterns repeatedly, find that the very process of change may become a distraction. Distraction may destroy true worship, yet what may be a distraction to one, may be an aid to worship for another.

Worship patterns, whether new or old, must be evaluated in terms of whether they aid or hinder an encounter of the people with the living God, whether they reveal or obscure the presence of the living Christ, whether they draw people to or repel them from God's Word, whether they lead toward or away from greater obedience to the Holy Spirit, and whether they equip and motivate people for mission.

The Church Gathers for Encouragement and Fellowship

In Hebrews 10:9-25 it becomes clear that the question about the importance of Christian assembly arose in the first century. Some apparently began to withdraw from the gatherings, though the reason for this is not given. The response to withdrawal was a strong admonition to Christians to continue to gather together:

> "Let us hold fast the confession of our hope without wavering, for he who promised is faithful; and let us consider how to stir up one another to love and good works, not neglecting to meet together, as is the habit of some, but encouraging one another, and all the more as you see the Day drawing near." Hebrews 10: 23-25

It is of interest that in the larger context here the writer speaks of faith, of hope, and of love. The implication is that one of the purposes of the assembly of Christians is that they may encourage each other in their faith, in their hope, and in the concrete exercise of love.

The idea of encouragement is basic here. The Greek word for encouragement in the Hebrews passage is used elsewhere of the ministry of the Holy Spirit. It includes the idea of standing at the side of another as a helper, being a counselor to another, or becoming an advocate for another. In secular usage, it was applied to the encouragement given to men in an army, just before going into battle. It means then, to stand by the side of another, putting one's hand on his shoulder, and giving him encouragement as he goes back into life's battles to witness and to serve.

This gives us another clue as to the purpose of our gathering. Christians need one another for mutual encouragement that they may be strengthened both in the presence of the temptations which they face and also in preparation for the tasks to be done. This gives substance to meeting for fellowship. This is basic to being a community, a *koinonia* (fellowship).

It is in the gathering of the congregation for fellowship that forgiveness and reconciliation among members in their relationship to each other must take place. Unless the congregation is itself a fellowship of the reconciled, it will be hindered in being an agent of reconciliation in the world.

The Church Gathers for Nurture and Dialogue

Even as the early church met to be instructed in "the apostles' teaching" concerning the meaning of the death and resurrection of Jesus Christ, and as they sought to discern the implications of this for their own lives, so the church in every generation needs to continue to gather for nurture. Broadly, this is what has been called the function of Christian education.

Paul Mininger has said that "Christian education in its broadest sense is the process by which the Christian community under a commission of Christ uses all its resources to restore man to the image of God and prepare him for expressing in all his relationships the cultural implications of the lordship of Christ."[4]

In 1963 the education commissions of the Mennonite Church and the General Conference Mennonite Church formulated and adopted the following objective for Christian education in our time:

"Through Christian education the church seeks to help all persons *to know God* as revealed supremely in Jesus Christ and the Scriptures:

to *become aware* of who they are,
      of what their situation is, and
      of their alienation to the end

that they may *repent* of their sin,
      respond to God's redeeming love in faith, and
      become members of the body of Christ;

81

to *grow* in Christ within the community of believers,
to walk in the Spirit in every relationship,
to fulfill the call to discipleship in the world, and
to abide in the Christian hope."

From these broad statements of the meaning and objective of Christian nurture, it is clear that instruction in the sense of sharing information is but one dimension. Nurture in this comprehensive sense involves all age levels in the life of the congregation. Normally, it includes the families of congregational members, but ought not be limited to these. The New Testament record indicates that unbelievers attended the gatherings of the early Christians (1 Cor. 14). One of the responsibilities which the gathered church has in view of the presence of those who do not understand or believe the Christian message is to make the gospel intelligible.

This, in turn, calls not only for an understanding of the characteristics of various age levels of children and youth in the church, but also an understanding of contemporary thought forms, of current vocabulary, and even more significantly of the deep questions which are in the minds of the people. This means that Christians must learn to listen in order that they, in turn, may learn to speak. The whole process of Christian nurture is deeply concerned with the problems of communication.

Implied in this broad understanding of nurture is the practice of discipline. This has both personal and group dimensions. Christians need each other both to sense the will of God more clearly and to become obedient to it. Church discipline takes many forms, including personal counseling and admonition, and sometimes group confrontation, but its purpose is always the restoration of the offender and the strengthening of the fellowship. The basic spirit and pattern is described in Matthew 18.

The Church Also Gathers for Discernment and Decision-making.

This may be seen simply as a further extension of the worship, fellowship, and nurture functions of the gathered church.

By discernment is meant the careful corporate search for the leading of God on a given here-and-now issue. The issue may involve an individual decision of some member of the group or it may involve a group decision.

Discernment in the Christian community takes place in a setting in which the Holy Spirit speaks through His Word and the Christian community is intelligently aware of the issues involved in the problem at hand.

The processes of discernment and decision-making involve careful study, open dialogue, and a moving in the direction of a consensus of the gathered congregation. Sometimes this is hard to achieve. Sometimes the failure to achieve consensus is due to lack of adequate study, sometimes to barriers to open communication, and sometimes it is a matter of insensitivity to the leading of the Holy Spirit, either on the part of the group as a whole or on the part of a few individuals.

Issues on which discernment and decisions are needed may be of many different kinds. There may be a question about beginning some new work as a congregation or conference, questions about commissioning persons for various ministries, questions concerning how to help each other more effectively in personal and community problems, questions pertaining to the planning of corporate ministries, questions pertaining to the use of resources available, or perhaps the discovery of new resources for tasks which are seen.

Traditionally, meetings for discernment and decision-making have been called the business meetings of congregations. The decline of their vitality in many congregations is a mark of decadence. Too often these meetings for discernment and decision-making have been removed too far from the worship, fellowship, and nurture functions of the congregation. They need to be seen as a part of the whole. Frequently the quality of the *koinonia* (fellowship) which exists in the congregation is reflected most clearly in meetings for discernment and decision-making. The quality of the *koinonia* in turn depends greatly on the intimacy of a congregation with its living Lord Jesus Christ, and on the serious application of mutual forgiveness and reconciliation in the local fellowship.

Whenever believers gather, questions concerning leadership responsibilities arise. We have already observed that in the history of the church there has been a tendency to centralize leadership and make this the responsibility of a very small group of persons. We have noted that the basic division of the church into two groups, one of which is called the clergy and the other of which is called the laity, is unbiblical. Yet the concept of leadership within Israel in the Old Testament and in the church of the New Testament is sociologically necessary and theologically approved. To see the responsibility of a whole congregation in the life and mission of the church in a proper relationship to the responsibilities of designated leaders is one of our tasks.

1. According to the biblical understanding, Christian ministry is the responsibility of "the whole people of God," the entire laity. The church's ministry is, therefore, a shared ministry. All are called to make Christ known. All are called to be participants in the Christian fellowship. All are called to serve in love.

2. In order that the church as a whole may fulfill its ministry, God endows with spiritual gifts certain persons from within the church for particular ministries to be servant-leaders of the larger body. Some are called to preaching-teaching ministries, some to pastoral counseling ministries, some to administrative tasks, and some may be commissioned by a congregation or conference for specific tasks in other places.

3. Sometimes various of these functions are combined in one person in a local congergation. Such a person may be called a pastor and may receive special ordination for his task. In recent years there has been much discussion on the role of pastors. Basic in the discussion has been the observation that congregations have placed too much responsibility into the hands of pastors and thus have expected more of them than was biblical, or possible. Particularly in a transition from the unsalaried to the salaried ministry, congregations have overburdened pastors with tasks with the feeling that he is "the one being paid" for this work. In the

process, congregations have tried to escape their own responsibilities for ministry. Both for the sake of congregations and pastors, the need has arisen to redefine the role of pastors in local congregations.[5]

4. According to Ephesians 4:11, 12, the purpose of leaders of various kinds in a local congregation is to equip the entire congregation for its ministry in the world. While local congregational situations may vary greatly from one another and, therefore, the role of a pastor also may vary from one situation to another, pastors are usually best qualified to serve as preacher-teachers of the Word. This ministry of proclamation and exposition of the divine Word calls for careful preparation and a gift of discernment which is of the Holy Spirit.

5. In the exercise of his role, however, a primary concern of the pastor is to help the congregation discern the gifts of its members; to encourage the dedication of these gifts to the Lord for service so that not only the entire congregation, but also the world may benefit from that which God has entrusted to an individual person; and to guide in the development of such gifts so that their usefulness may be enhanced. This dimension of the pastor's task calls for intimate acquaintance with members of the congregation, for his participation in dialogue with family and other small groups, and the development of warm personal relationships which will make it possible for him to become a kind of "catalyst-counselor" in personal and small group situations.

6. The posture of the pastor, however, is always that of the servant. Whatever scope and shape his particular leadership responsibilities in a local congregation may take—depending on his own gifts and those possessed by others, the size of the congregation, the stage of spiritual development, and particularly the needs of the community in which the congregation is located—it will always be the aim of the pastor to share his leadership responsibility with others so that in fact, and not only in theory, the congregation as a whole may be involved in ministry. Even in his particular role as preacher-teacher, he seeks to help others also to learn how better to interpret the Scriptures, how better

to discern the Word of God for our times, and how better to communicate in public and private ways.

GATHERING AS PREPARATION FOR SCATTERING

When the congregation gathers for such functions as have been mentioned, namely, worship, fellowship, nurture, and decision-making, it is important to keep these functions in a clear relationship to the "outward journey" or the mission of the church. Christians must guard diligently against permitting their gathering to become an end in itself. Critics of the church have some justification in their observation that for many churchgoers Christianity is contained within the walls of a church building. Congregations which construct ornate and extravagant church buildings, spend the largest percentage of their material resources on their own local worship and nurture programs, and are "always willing, but never able" to help in the cause of world missions, Christian relief ministries, or Christian social action causes, undermine the credibility of the Christian cause in the world.

Trueblood properly insists:

> "The Church is a particular fellowship of men and women involved in common life, sharing the life of Christ, who assemble with one another for the purpose of *sending*. Christians are perpetually being "sent out" (Mark 6:7), but they cannot be sent out unless they have already been *drawn in*. The Christian operation, which never ends, is that according to which Disciples are continually being turned into Apostles, but members must be Disciples first. What is the use of being sent out if men have nothing to give when they arrive? How can dialogue with the world be worth anything if the saints have nothing to say?"[6]

In view of this, congregations need to reevaluate their patterns of gathering to determine whether or not they are sufficiently "geared for mission." Not only should meetings of the gathered congregation be the occasion for the promotion of mission and relief offerings, but they should provide opportunity for people to wrestle vigorously with the question of what they, as individuals and as a corporate group, can do and ought to do in mission in the local community in which God has placed them. Though the church's mission does not end "in Jerusalem," it begins there.

86

Not only should *motivation* for personal and corporate Christian witness and service be provided, but also *instruction, understanding,* and the development of *skills* to make such witness and service more meaningful and effective. It is not without reason that many members of congregations report that when they gather for meetings of the local church, they are greatly stimulated to do something in the matter of witnessing to the unsaved or serving the needy. However, often they leave meetings of the church quite frustrated because they have received no light on how to respond practically to the appeals which have been made. Efforts which are put forth on a purely individual basis often fail with the result that the Christian becomes discouraged because he does not know how to take his place in mission. To inspire persons to witness and serve without giving them help in obedience is to be irresponsible in Christian teaching and Christian mission.

The gathering of the congregation, then, needs to be seen in the context of the church's mission. Not only do Christians go from the "worship-study-discernment" gatherings into their ministries of witness and service in the world, but they come back into the gathered congregation with certain kinds of experiences which they have had out in the world. Some of these experiences have been encouraging and become the basis for testimony and praise. Other experiences have been disappointing and become the basis for further study and more prayer.

The point is, that there should be a vital link between that which Christians experience in their attempt to fulfill their part of the church's ministry and that which happens in the meetings of the gathered congregation itself. This calls for Spirit-led leadership and responsible participation at all levels of the life of the gathered church.

1 Elizabeth O'Connor, *Journey Inward, Journey Outward* (New York: Harper and Row, 1968), p. ix.
2 Elton Trueblood, *The Incendiary Fellowship* (New York: Harper and Row, 1967), p. 83.
3 Eduard Schweizer, *Church Order in the New Testament* (Naperville, Illinois: Alec R. Allenson, Inc., 1961), pp. 221-223.
4 Paul Mininger, "Culture for Service," *The Mennonite Quarterly Review,* January 1955, pp. 10, 11.
5 A helpful restatement is Paul M. Miller, *Servant of God's Servants* (Scottdale, Pennsylvania: Herald Press, 1964).
6 Trueblood, *op. cit.,* p. 83.

Chapter 8

The Church Scattered

In 1964 George W. Webber of the East Harlem Protestant Parish in New York published a book entitled *The Congregation in Mission*.[1] It was based in part on his own experience in city ministries and in part on his biblical studies and reflection on them. This book seeks to describe a city congregation as it attempts to take seriously its mandate to mission in the metropolis. It recognizes that there must be a solid congregational base from which this mission radiates. It stresses the necessity of mission as that which gives the gathered congregation a reason for existence and an agenda for its meetings. It insists that the congregations must develop "missionary structures" which are appropriate to their situation and relevant to modern need. It moves on the conviction that "the church exists for mission."

One year later, Wallace E. Fisher wrote a book entitled *From Tradition to Mission* in which he described the process through which a congregation in Lancaster, Pennsylvania, found new meaning in their existence as a city church.[2] He describes dramatically the struggles which were involved in moving from "a traditional church" to a people of God actively involved in mission in the city.

Scattering as Judgment and Opportunity

To speak of the church as scattered, is to speak of the church in mission. It is noteworthy that the idea of scattering in the Bible was not first related to mission, and only in a secondary way became the occasion for mission. In the Old Testament the idea of scattering is frequently associated with judgment and tragedy (Gen. 11:9; Ex. 5:2; Lev. 26:33; Deut. 4:27; etc.). Even Jesus spoke of the tragedy of people being like scattered sheep without a shepherd (Mt. 9:36; 26:31). So also the Book of Acts records the "scattering" of the church of Jerusalem (Acts 8:1) through "great persecution." Immediately thereafter, however, it introduces the idea of mission. "Now those who were scattered went about preaching the word" (Acts 8:4). This is the simplest biblical description of the scattered church at work in mission.

Acts 11:19-26 reports that this scattering, being the occasion of the preaching of the Word, resulted in the establishment of a new congregation at Antioch. The church at Antioch, according to Acts, became the hub of great new missionary activity, taking the gospel into Asia Minor and Europe. First Peter also speaks of Christians as scattered and links their experience of persecution while they live as aliens and strangers in a hostile society with the opportunity to witness for Christ, always ready to give a reason for the hope that lies in them (1 Pet. 1:1; 3:15).

The scattering of the people of God in history, then has meant both judgment and opportunity. In this lesson "the church scattered" means the church responding to its opportunities for mission, whether in the immediate locality or in the world in a larger, national, or even global sense.

It is not possible to describe all of the dimensions of the life and activity of the church scattered. Our attention will be focused on two dimensions related to two different levels of the life of the church. At the level of the local congregation, the scattered church represents for us the members of the congregation in their homes, in their neighborhoods, in their community relationships, in schools, in their occupational life, in their recreation, their travel, or perchance, on special assignments which they fulfill outside of the actual meeting of the local congregation of believers.

At the level of the conference life, the scattered church is found in missionary appointments of various kinds, peace witness and relief assignments, voluntary service ministries of many kinds, institutional ministries whether of an educational, a therapeutic, a custodial, or rehabilitating nature.

While it is recognized that Christians involved in ministries in the world in these various ways may come together in many different kinds of subgroups, such as an institutional staff meeting, a voluntary service unit meeting, or a mission staff meeting, it is their witnessing and service activities which are primary in our consideration in this chapter.

VARIETIES OF MINISTRIES: WITNESS AND SERVICE

In chapter three attention was given to the relationship between evangelism and social action as two foci of the ministry of the church in the world. It was emphasized that while each has a proper claim on the responsibility of the Christian church, the two need to be seen in relationship to each other and a balance in emphasis is imperative. In this chapter, as we speak of varieties of ministries, both the witnessing and the serving dimensions are to be kept in view. It is scarcely helpful to identify certain forms of ministry as being more of a witness than others, while other forms may be more of the service type. Essentially in the perspective we have adopted in these studies, all ministries should embody a quality of *witness* and all should partake of the spirit and quality of *service*.

Congregational Ministries

Among the more familiar patterns of congregational outreach for witness and service are the following: inviting neighbors to participate in worship, fellowship, or educational activities of the local congregation; establishing church-sponsored vacation schools, nursery schools, or day nurseries for children of working mothers; sponsoring community recreational programs and camping programs for the underprivileged; conducting worship and/or evangelistic services in homes, hospitals, or prisons; distributing Christian literature in appropriate situations to persons who would otherwise not receive it; and sponsoring service projects to help needy persons in the community. In addition to these common forms of group activity, Christians become involved in a vast number of personal conversations and person-to-person ministries which have some witness or service quality. Much of what is done needs to be reevaluated in terms of motivation, meaning, and impact. Some of these forms continue to have real value.

The possibilities for witness and service are much more numerous and have larger dimensions than most congregations realize. To focus attention on the larger range of possibilities for congregational ministries, it is helpful to identify various kinds of "communities" to which the Christian community may relate itself for purposes of ministry. This list of potential community relationships is probably more typical of the town-and-country situation than of an inner city. The various kinds of community are simply identified in outline form in order to suggest the great variety of possible ways in which a local ministering community may become active. The involvement may be on an individual, small group, or congregational basis. It is obvious that a local congregation would need to evaluate carefully the legitimacy of each type of involvement, the kind of involvement which should be developed, and what the priorities should be. It would be quite impossible to state universal principles which would apply to all situations. It would be the province of the local congregation as a "congregation of discernment and decision-making" to determine which relationships hold greatest potential.

1. The Religious Community
    Ministerial associations: varieties based on geographical and political units; denominational groupings; theological emphases
    Other religious organizations
        Councils of churches
        YMCA and YWCA organizations
        Evangelistic organizations
        Specialized interest groups: rescue missions, Youth for Christ

2. The Therapeutic Community
    Relation to doctors: medical and psychiatric
    Relation to hospitals: general and psychiatric

3. The Helping Community (other than medical and psychiatric)

Social welfare agencies: (private and public) family service agencies, adult and child guidance clinics, rehabilitation centers, agencies for unwed mothers

Employment agencies

Homes for the aged; senior citizens' communities

Legal counsel

Alcoholics Anonymous

Funeral directors

4. The Political Community

Relation to law enforcement agencies: work with juvenile delinquents, with courts, with penal institutions, with those in prison and those on parole

Relation to county and city government agencies: city planning, zoning commissions, rural and urban renewal projects

Relation to partisan politics: encouragement of voting, analysis of political issues, and other types of involvement

5. The Educational Community

The parochial school: Roman Catholic, Protestant

The public school: relationship to administrators, teachers, school programs, standards, teacher selection, reorganization and development programs

The public library: making use of it; participation in development

The cultural organizations: lectureships, music, drama clubs

The scouting program

6. The Commercial Community

Relationships to commercial and/or rural community leaders (banks, real estate, business, industry)

Relationships to organizations: Chamber of Commerce, Junior Chamber of Commerce, service clubs, and farmers' organizations

Community celebrations: parades, exhibits

7. The Laboring Community

Each member's own employment situation

Relation to labor organizations
Relation to management

8. The Recreational Community
Y activities and programs
Local athletic organizations

9. The "Communicating" Community
Relation to local editors, radio personnel, television personnel
Use of local news media
Possibilities for witness

10. The Unchurched Community
Individuals and families with no meaningful church relationships
The new resident
The nominal church member
The hard-core antagonist of the church

Denominational Ministries

In addition to the vast variety of possible ministries for the congregation as it *scatters* into the local community, we need to think of another large category of ministries which generally take place at the level of denominational agencies and sometimes on interdenominational bases.

There are many different ways of grouping such ministries. One of these is as follows:[3]

1. Ministries Through Institutions: educational, hospital, penal, and custodial, such as "homes" of various kinds.

These ministries are as diverse as the various kinds of institutions represented. Within each of these institutions there will in turn be a variety of ministries. Basically these ministries may be seen as part of "the church scattered," organizing itself along lines of specialized services, planning programs carefully, developing facilities, recruiting and preparing personnel, and thus seeking to meet the needs of persons out of Christian motivation and with high professional competence.

2. Ministries to Business and Industry

This is a newer form of ministry which is concerned about more than chaplaincy relationships to individuals who work in business and industrial firms. While some kinds of industrial ministry focus on persons, other types focus on the structures of management, labor, sales, research, and development.

Persons who become involved in ministries of this kind will be concerned about what is happening to executives and those related to them. However, there will also be a concern about ethical issues involved in the development and conduct of the company. Such questions as fair wages, proper working conditions, and good working relationships are but a part of Christian concern. Deeper issues such as the ethics of salesmanship, of advertising, price fixing, and the effects of automation, new research, and the offering of new products to the public—all become a part of the agenda of Christians who seek to minister in this area.

3. Ministry Through Political Processes

The area of a peace witness to the government is already familiar to churches of the Anabaptist-Mennonite heritage. Increasingly, however, the concern for civil-rights legislation and other forms of political activity have become a deep concern to Christian communities.

Ministries to the higher levels of government can usually best be carried out from denominational and interdenominational bases rather than from the local congregation. This does not eliminate the possibility that a local congregation may wish to express its concerns to congressmen and in this way become involved in this type of ministry. This is a complicated form of Christian ministry about which there is much difference of conviction among Christians.

4. Crisis Ministries

Familiar forms are those which are occasioned by war, by racial conflict, or by an exploding population. These call for special forms of Christian ministry which are usually developed on an interim basis.

This type of ministry in the world illustrates the fact that the church must be ready to respond to the needs of the times. When the crisis which occasions such ministries has passed, it is assumed that these ministries then are discontinued so that other new needs may be met.

Among Mennonites some of the ministries carried on by the Mennonite Central Committee would illustrate this type. Feeding the famine victims in India, providing blankets for war refugees in Vietnam and in Jordan, or helping to build houses for the homeless in postwar Germany, would be examples.

5. Ministries Through the Arts

Relatively little attention has been given to special Christian ministries through literature, art, and drama. In a culture in which the fine arts have a very significant role, in which their power is expressed through the printed page, the television screen, and the public platform, Christians cannot ignore this opportunity for ministry. In this area, also, it is likely that such ministries can best be opened and developed at denominational agency levels.

THE WHOLE PEOPLE INVOLVED IN WITNESS AND SERVICE

Having surveyed very briefly and by no means exhaustively a number of different fronts on which the scattered church may minister in the world, giving witness and service "in the Name of Christ," we already recognize the vastness and multiplicity of such opportunities. It becomes clear that if a congregation thinks in terms of fulfilling its ministry to the world through one person whom they may call the pastor, it will be totally impossible for the church to fulfill its obligations on these many fronts. This, in fact, is what has been wrong in too many cases. Christians have thought of their ministry to the world as being the responsibility of one person in each congregation, rather than being the responsibility of the whole membership.

If one begins to consider the total resources which are represented in the membership of a congregation, one recognizes that it is possible to exert a Christian witness on many of these fronts.

When a local congregation begins to take inventory of its own personnel resources for witness and service, people will be amazed at the number of fronts at which this ministry is possible. One may also be surprised at the resources in education and experience as well as personal spiritual gifts which are represented in the membership.

Beyond this, of course, denominational administrators carry the responsibility of surveying the resources in the larger brotherhood to determine what may be available in terms of personnel and financial resources as well as experience and insight to establish and develop ministries on the larger frontiers of economic, political, and the esthetic life. While it may still be true that the total resources of the church may seem small in comparison to the need for Christian witness and service in the world, it should be clear that when the total resources of the brotherhood are recognized and mobilized, a vastly increased ministry becomes a possibility.

D. L. Moody is often quoted as having said at one point in his life, "The world has yet to see what God can do with one man whose life is wholly dedicated to Him. By the grace of God, I will be that man." In a somewhat parallel way, it could be said, "The world has yet to see what God can do with a congregation (or denomination) which is wholly dedicated to Him." Surely, the dedication of a group which would match in quality the dedication of D. L. Moody, would become the occasion of an overwhelming renewal of Christian witness and service in our time.

ORGANIZING FOR WITNESS AND SERVICE

Having noted many varieties of ministries which are open to Christian groups today and having reflected on the great resources which are to be found in the whole Christian brotherhood, empowered by the Holy Spirit, we still need to consider the practical question of organization for witness and service.

Here we face two conflicting points of view, both of which may be partly in error. On the one hand, there are the anti-organization people who argue that the church has been failing in the past because it has substituted organization for the Holy Spirit. They argue that if you want to see God work, you must avoid organizational structures as much as possible. Some go so far as to say that organization always gets in the way of effective ministry.

On the other hand, we have the pro-organization people who tend to feel that the Holy Spirit can always do His best work when things are most clearly and efficiently organized. Such persons are preoccupied with organization charts which show clearly the lines of authority, the delegation of responsibility, and the precise channels for communication. Using models from business and industry and at times even borrowing from the military organization, such persons in all sincerity may insist that in order to get the work of the church done, we must have the best possible form of church organization and administration.

The truth seems to be that the Holy Spirit is able to work both through church organization and also outside it. He works through carefully structured programs, but also through the more spontaneous and less carefully planned ministries. When these are motivated by Christian love, they may reach the hearts of people and meet their personal needs in a remarkably effective way. Samuel Shoemaker is right when he says that we do well to think of God as having two hands, the one represented by the conventional well-organized church, and the other by the more spontaneous, free and experimental ministries. When these two can work in cooperation with each other rather than being in competition, then, as he says, we have "the whole church."

Church organization and administration are functions not to be depreciated. In fact, continuity in ministry makes some form of organization and administration essential. Church administration has been defined as "the task of helping the congregation (or denomination) as a whole, as well as individual Christians to discover, develop, and utilize for witness and service the resources which God has granted, whether charismatic spiritual gifts, material resources, persons, or time. Administration makes it possible for the congregation (or denomination) to do together what individuals (or congregations), not constructively related to each other, could not do in the fulfillment of the mission of the church.

The question of the extent to which the pastor of the local congregation should become involved in church administration must be considered in each situation. What is important is that this task be carried by competent and responsible persons. It is clear that an efficient organization-minded leader, without the cooperation of a congregation, can do very little in the area of witness and service. It is also true, however, that a congregation of willing, though not always competent, persons will likewise fail to realize its potential for witness and service unless someone is able to give creative and challenging organizational leadership.

Whatever forms Christian witness and service may take in the local community or in the world, and however the church may need to organize to fulfill its ministry, this must always be prophetic, redemptive, and loving. It must be prophetic in that it calls attention to God's purpose and to His judgments. It must be redemptive in that it bears witness to Jesus Christ who is Redeemer, Reconciler, Savior, and Lord. It is done "in His Name." It must be loving because this is the essence of service (*diakonia*) which is simply an incarnating of the love of God being shed abroad in the world. When organizational patterns begin to interfere with the communication of love as the heart of witness and service, they need to be reevaluated and revised. Church organization should serve as a vehicle through which God's love for persons is given better opportunity to become known and operative. It fails when it becomes a barrier to the communication of the love of Christ which motivates the church.

1 George W. Webber, *The Congregation in Mission* (Nashville: Abingdon Press, 1964).

2 Wallace E. Fisher, *From Tradition to Mission* (New York: Abingdon Press, 1965).

3 This is adapted from *Theological Education,* Spring 1968, p. 696, published by the American Association of Theological Schools, 534 Third National Building, Dayton, Ohio 45402.

Chapter 9

Seeking Relevance

> Perhaps the best argument for changing the structures of Protestantism is that the present form of the church seems unable to speak to the outside, or to vitally involve those who are already on the inside.[1]

Some of the criticism of the church in our time is unfair. Some does not apply to the congregations of which we are a part. However, the volume, variety, and persistence of the criticism of the church expressed in our time would make it fatal if the church were to ignore it. Criticism needs to be faced, evaluated, and dealt with wherever possible.

Common Criticisms

Here are some of the common criticisms which are made again and again, not simply by carping faultfinders, but by responsible and concerned persons, some of whom are outside of the organized church, but most of whom are members "on the inside."

1. The church is irrelevant to contemporary human problems both 1) to the burning social issues of war and peace, racial conflict, and poverty, and 2) to the deep personal, psychological, and family problems which modern man faces. The social issues are being left to the universities and to the politicians. The personal problems are turned over to family counselors and to the psychiatrists.

2. It is not involved "where the action is." It is introverted and withdrawn to "the comfortable pew" (Pierre Berton), or to the comfortable small group where in dialogue each helps to bolster the bruised ego of the other.

3. It is muscle-bound by tradition, living in a world of the

past, not alert to the changes taking place in the contemporary world. It is "sleeping through the modern revolution." It accepts change only when it has to, when there is no longer any other alternative, and then usually too little and too late.

4. It is not communicating to the modern world. Neither its theological concepts nor its vocabulary are any longer understood. It uses media which are antiquated. It preaches, pontificates, and makes pronouncements, but no one is really listening, nor would they understand if they were listening. Its points of contact are forced, unnatural, or nonexistent.

5. Its structures are not geared for mission. Churches are building-oriented, clergy-oriented, and organization-oriented rather than person-oriented and mission-oriented.

6. It is divided, theologically and denominationally, unable to give a united witness to a fragmented world, or to deal with its own internal or external problems with the strength of unity. A divided house, as Jesus recognized, is not only weak. It disintegrates.

While there are additional criticisms, these gather up much of what is being said. If one were to summarize these, the idea of irrelevance would be basic to most of them. One of the signs of hope in our time is that in response to its own study of the Word, and because of its capacity to hear criticism, the church is today "seeking relevance."

But What Is Relevance?

The dictionary definition of *relevant* is, "bearing on the matter at hand," "pertinent," having "a traceable, significant, logical connection." For the church to be seeking relevance, then, means that it is attempting 1) to hear the deep and real questions which people are asking, 2) to sense the authentic rather than merely the articulated or imagined needs, and 3) to respond in word and deed, to these genuine needs in language which is understandable and in action which has meaning. It means that the church is seeking diligently to rediscover or reestablish "a traceable, significant, logical connection" between the Christian message and people's deep needs, between the church's institutions and contemporary problems, between its own programs and what is going on in today's world.

Sometimes relevance has been defined as "answering the real questions people are asking." On the surface this is helpful for it is clear that sometimes the church has been answering questions which no one was asking. However, this analysis needs further probing. If it is said that the church has been answering the wrong questions, do we know that people today are asking the right questions?

Relevance and Questions

As a matter of fact, which are the "right questions"? Are they those which the psychiatrist hears? Are they those which the anthropologist hears? Or the public opinion pollster? If in all these surveys, no one is really asking explicitly about Jesus Christ and the Word of God, would this mean that Christ is no longer relevant to modern man? Would this mean that He no longer really matters? Would it mean that modern man has indeed "come of age," and that he has outgrown his need for God and salvation and eternal life? And what about forgiveness and regeneration and reconciliation?

Too few of the contemporary discussions on the issue of relevance give adequate consideration to the problem of man's sinfulness. Too often they overlook the capacity of man to hide himself not only from others but also from his conscious self. Even as professional counselors are wary of the diagnoses that clients make of their own troubles, the church may need to be wary of the diagnoses which men of the world make of their problems. It is by no means to be taken for granted that men really need what they think they need, or what they say they need. Hiding from one's self, from others, and from God is one of the most persistent characteristics of man in every generation. The truth is that what men may consider most irrelevant to their situation, may be precisely what is needed most.

Relevance and Christ

From the perspective of Christian faith then, the discovery of true relevance cannot be made apart from the revelation of God in Jesus Christ. This revelation is made most explicit in "God's Word written," but needs to be understood in the light of the Holy Spirit who can also help the contemporary church to recognize and interpret what modern man is asking, thinking, feeling, or needing. Moreover, the establishment of the point of contact and the maintenance of genuine dialogue between those "on the inside" of the church and those "on the outside" is a miracle made possible through the working of the Holy Spirit. This is not to say that there is nothing the church can do to become relevant. As a matter of fact, there is much that the church must do.

While there is wide agreement that the church in our time must seek greater relevance, there is not the same agreement as to the nature of true relevance or as to how this is to be found. Everyone agrees that the way to greater relevance is renewal in some form. But what kind of renewal do we need and by what means is it realized?

THE RENEWAL OF THE CHURCH

Christ and Change

Those who fear change in the world and in the church have often found Hebrews 13:8 as a great comfort, "Jesus Christ is the same yesterday, today, and for ever." Theodore H. Robinson has called this one of the greatest single sentences in the New Testament. "It is the knowledge of the fact therein stated which gives the human soul its certainty, the church its continuity, and both a solid foundation on which they can be built up."[2] It was addressed to Christians originally who themselves were facing the impact and implications of change. They had changed from Judaism to Christianity and needed to be reassured of the stabilizing reality in Jesus Christ who is always the same.

More careful reflection on this passage, however, reminds us that Jesus Christ is not only a stabilizer in change. He is Himself an initiator of change. Jesus Christ who is the same in our experience as He was in the Gospels, has a good deal to say about regeneration, which is personal change; and about the kingdom of God being at hand, which involves tremendous social change. If this same Jesus Christ is Lord both of the individual and of history, we cannot be His true disciples without being subjected continually to the changes which He is seeking to bring about in us, in the church, and in the world.

The renewal of the church, then, is a form of change. From the Christian perspective, it needs to be understood as change which Christ Himself through the working of His Holy Spirit is seeking to bring to pass. The issue is not so much whether the church is keeping up with the changing times as it is a question of whether it is keeping up with Jesus Christ and His Holy Spirit, alive and active in today's world.

The basic problem for most Christians is probably not to accept the fact of change, but it is to know what kind of change is really "of the Lord" and how such change can be brought about without bringing alienation and schism into the fellowship. Complicating the situation is the fact that prophets of renewal do not all give us the same formulas.

Formulas of Renewal

1. One kind of formula for the revitalization of the contemporary church focuses on the *renewal of persons*. It is said that we need a greater dedication to evangelism and that renewal comes only through personal conversion and a recommitment of life to the Lord. It is emphasized that we need a renewal of the life of prayer which has become dormant and meaningless in the lives of many Christians. It is stressed that we need a deepening of the quality of Christian commitment so that as persons become members of Christian congregations, it is clear to them and to everyone that to be a participating Christian in our time means that one belongs to "the company of the committed" (Elton Trueblood). Again it is said that renewal comes only through a new work of

the Holy Spirit and that this, in turn, comes only through intense asking, through "full surrender," and a complete willingness to receive "whatever gift God gives."

2. Others would prescribe formulas for the revitalization of the church which focus on the *renewal of the congregational life.*

1) Among these are those who plead for a *renewal of preaching,* insisting that this involves not only a new understanding of the nature of preaching and a new dedication to it, but also the involvement of the congregation in the selection of preaching themes, in corporate Bible study of the passages which are the basis of preaching, and in the search for the concrete application of the Word in the contemporary situation.

2) Others see the renewal of the congregation coming through *new forms of worship and liturgy.* They are given to experimentation with modern musical settings for the confessions of the church. They would utilize modern art forms. Some would include bodily motion as part of worship patterns. They would recognize the contributions which contemporary architecture can make to help modern man in his worship. They would put the confessions and prayers in the contemporary idiom and so would seek to make meaningful to the new generation the eternal truths of the gospel.

3) Others would plead for the development of dynamic small groups, sometimes called *koinonia* groups, as a channel of revitalization for the local congregation. Such groups may be study groups, prayer groups, personal sharing groups, or witness or service groups. What they have in common is that they bring a small number of persons, usually from seven to twelve, together in a face-to-face situation. They accent the importance of the participation of every member of the group, and they seek both personal and congregational renewal.

4) Still others would insist that the renewal of the congregation also requires a *restructuring of its organizational patterns.* It is argued that the congregation must take a new look at its particular mission and then develop "missionary structures" which make possible the fulfillment of this mission. It is generally assumed that the structures which exist are not adequate and, therefore,

organizational change is required. One dimension of this approach insists that the church needs to develop new forms of ministry which it had not been practicing in the past. These new forms are to minister to sectors of society which have either been overlooked by the church, which have newly come into being because of technological change or social change, or which for some reason have been estranged from the church.

3. In addition to the formulas which focus on the renewal of persons and on the renewal of the congregation, there are those which focus on *the renewal of society and of its structures in the world.*

They argue that the renewal of the church comes through a recognition of what God is doing in the world, and then "getting with it." They identify what God is doing with social reform movements which seek the alleviation of economic injustice, the elimination of racial discrimination, or some other form of improved social conditions. They see God at work in political developments, in some of the revolutionary movements, in legislation which promotes peace and equal opportunity. They see God at work in protest movements against the corrupt establishments of society.

Instead of the church becoming a resource and channel of renewal to the world, they would insist that God's activity in the world must become a resource for the renewal of the church. Instead of the sequence of renewal being: God-Church-World, they insist that the true sequence is: God-World-Church. It is quite clear that this approach differs from the ones described previously.

The consideration of these various formulas for renewal will call for careful study and spiritually-guided discernment and decision-making in local congregations and also by conference bodies. John Howard Yoder has called attention to the limitations of both the "pietistic" formulas for renewal with their focus on the personal dimensions of life, and also those of the "puritan" approach which is absorbed with "the reformation of society" seeking "to make history come out right." Those who are committed to the believers' church will be concerned with both individual persons and also with social justice. They will continue to find the congregation of believing persons as a significant base from which ministries, both to persons and to society, may find expression. The renewing work of God, to be sure, is not limited to local congregations or to denominational agencies. The issue which is being faced here is whether the renewal of the church in the sense of congregation and denomination is possible. To this we give a strong affirmative answer.

The Process of Renewal

The process of change, whether in the local congregation or in the denomination, includes at least five important steps.

1. The first of these is an *awareness of need*. Unless such awareness of need exists, not only on the part of a few individuals, but also on the part of a substantial number of members, there will not likely be a climate in which change is either desired or possible. Awareness of need comes through earnest and open-minded study of the Scriptures under the guidance of the Spirit. It also comes through a careful assessment of the situation in the contemporary world as well as of the conditions in the church.

2. A second step in the process of change is *dialogue*. Dialogue involves careful listening, honest speaking, and genuine dedication to discover and do the will of God on the part of the believing church. This dialogue must be carried on not only among members of the church but between members of the church and those who are on the outside.

3. A third step is *discernment*. This should be the outcome of true dialogue. This is the process of bringing together all that one has observed, sifting the true from the false, sensing what should have the priority, and moving toward decision. Essentially, it is the will of God which is to be discerned.

4. The fourth step is *action*. Change never takes place unless some decisions are made which are translated into action. Such action must be undertaken courageously but always responsibly.

5. A final element in the process of change should always be

reevaluation. Only Roman Catholicism in the past has held to a doctrine of "an infallible church." All forms of Protestantism, including the Mennonites, recognize that a fallible church can make changes which are contrary to the best interests of the brotherhood or to the will of God. Therefore, after action has been taken, the congregation must remain open to the possibility of having made a wrong decision and thus evaluation is necessary so that the error can be corrected and mistakes can be rectified.

THE ROLE OF EXPLORATION AND EXPERIMENTATION

What has been said about seeking relevance and the process of church renewal thus far, leads to some observations concerning the role of exploration and experimentation.

Congregations and denominations will find themselves facing pressures from those who would be very free to experiment with all kinds of new patterns as well as those who want to stay with the tried and the proven and therefore oppose experimentation. The following guidelines have been suggested to help give both theological sanction and also restraints in the matter of experimentation.[3]

1. Assuming that experimentation in some form is necessary in the congregation seeking renewal, Christ Himself is recognized as "the Lord of the experiment."

2. The experiment of the congregation aims to uncover some new territory. It wants God "to show the land." It makes explorations because there is "yet much land to be possessed."

3. Every experiment in the congregation, however, is "for keeps." Experimentation can never be "playing" in the sense of not being serious. It means that ultimate issues are at stake and that when in the experiment, Christ reveals new truth or makes a new mandate, we are committed to obey.

4. In experimentation we need to be conscious of limitations and avoid generalizations on the basis of limited experience or observation. The fact that a new form of worship is meaningful

in one situation does not mean that it is necessarily applicable to all congregations in a denomination.

5. No experiment ought to ignore what is already known. Before undertaking new patterns, there must be serious study of old patterns, of their history, of their meanings, and of their limitations.

6. There must be openness for continual revision. The possibility of failure must be built-in from the beginning in the sense that the questions with which the experiment started out may find a negative answer.

7. Experimentation must always be responsible. This demands the art of seeing what is going on and to understand what is seen. This means careful preparation, deep awareness of implications for persons and structures involved, and an openness to either positive or negative results.

As congregations and denominations become open to experimentation, they can learn a great deal from each other. It is just as important to know what has been tried and failed as it is to know of some new possibility that has not yet been tried. The approach of experimentation is a part of the scientific age and has tremendous possibilities for good if used properly by the church. Abuse of the experimental approach can lead to shallowness, superficiality, and destructive attitudes and practices.

1 Stephen Rose, *The Grass Roots Church* (New York: Holt, Rinehart and Winston, 1966), p. 29.

2 Theodore H. Robinson, *The Epistle to the Hebrews* (Naperville: Allenson, 1933), on this passage.

3 Adopted from a statement by Worner Simpfendoerfer in Thomas Wieser, ed., *Planning for Mission* (New York: The U. S. Conference for the World Council of Churches, 1966) pp. 153-156.

Chapter 10

The Hope and Vision of the Church

> The Christian community does not live from itself and for itself, but from the sovereignty of the Risen Lord and for the coming sovereignty of Him Who has conquered death and is bringing life, righteousness, and the Kingdom of God.[1]

In a profound sense the church is saved by hope (Rom. 8:24) and lives by hope (1 Pet. 1:3). When hope has died, the church has died. Hope along with faith and love, belongs to the essence of the church's being (1 Cor. 13:13). Hope in a biblical sense is not just a shaky aspiration. It is certainly not to be understood as a dream which can never be realized. In popular language the word *hope* is sometimes used in these ways. Hope, biblically understood, is "a sure and steadfast anchor of the soul" (Heb. 6:19) though its basis is not visible (Rom. 8:24; Heb. 11:1) and is, therefore, grasped by faith. In speaking of its hope, the church can never present unequivocal evidence, neither can it say, all the signs point in this direction. Christian hope does not find its ground in the human situation or in the evident course of human history.

The content of Christians' hope depends on the revelation of God in Christ as this is discerned through a Spirit-illuminated study of the Scriptures. Here and there in history and in personal experience, to be sure, the Christian may become aware of intimations that Christian hope is being realized. He may see the signs of the coming kingdom, giving him encouragement. Essentially, however, Christian hope is the work and gift of the Holy Spirit in and among His people.

It is not the purpose of this chapter to spell out the full range of Christian eschatology, that is, the teaching about "last things." Discussion of the differences between premillennialists, post-millennialists, and amillennialists belongs elsewhere. Neither is it possible here to deal in depth with the question of the tension which seems to exist within the New Testament itself, between those passages which emphasize universal judgment and separation, and those which seem to speak of universal redemption. What must be said emphatically, however, is that any view of the Christian hope which fails to take seriously both the judgment and the salvation of God, both His holiness and His love, both divine sovereignty and human freedom, has probably arrived at too easy a solution to the problem of human destiny.

We may consider here both the ultimate hope and also the mediate hope of the church. By the ultimate hope, we mean that which Scriptures project as the final destiny of the people of God. By the mediate hope of the church, we mean its apparent prospects for the foreseeable future. For the former we depend on biblical teaching. For the second we depend more on human judgment.

THE ULTIMATE HOPE: THE KINGDOM OF GOD

Strange as it may seem, the church's ultimate hope is for that which makes the church obsolete and unnecessary. The church's hope is for its own elimination. Parodoxically and profoundly, the church is not interested in its own survival. Ideally this should be true in a local, denominational, and even universal sense.

The Church and the Kingdom

From the perspective of the New Testament, the "aeon of the church" lies between the resurrection of Jesus Christ and His Parousia. The church, as Paul Erb puts it, "has something of an interim character."[2] During this interim, it has work to do. It has a witness to give and a service to render "until He come."

110

The hope and vision of the church is ultimately the kingdom of God. This, as envisioned by Old Testament prophets, as proclaimed by Jesus Christ Himself, and as confessed by the early church involves the perfect rule of God.

> Then comes the end, when he delivers the kingdom to God the Father after destroying every rule and every authority and power . . . . When all things are subjected to him, then the Son himself will also be subjected to him who put all things under him, that God may be everything to every one. 1 Corinthians 15:24-28

In essence this is the vision which the Old Testament prophets had of a situation of perfect *Shalom* (Is. 2:1-10; Mic. 4:1-5). It is that kingdom of God which Jesus proclaimed as being at hand (Mk. 1:15). In the presence of the king entering into the world, this was being fulfilled. It is also that for which He taught the disciples to pray, "Thy kingdom come, Thy will be done on earth as it is in heaven" (Mt. 6:10). It is essentially that of which we read in Ephesians of how God purposes in Christ in the fullness of time "to unite all things in him, things in heaven and things on earth" (Eph. 1:9). The gift of the Holy Spirit working in the church is given as "the guarantee of our inheritance" (Eph. 1:14). It is that for which "the whole creation has been groaning in travail" . . . to "be set free from its bondage to decay and obtain the glorious liberty of the children of God" (Rom. 8:21, 22).

From these passages it is clear that the coming of the kingdom is not portrayed simply as the consummation of the church, but that it is the completion of humanity and of all creation. It is not only a condition of perfect reconciliation but a fulfillment of God's purpose for men, nations, and history.

Christ and the Kingdom

Central to this portrayal of the hope of the church in the New Testament is the *Parousia* (coming and presence) of the lord of the church, even Jesus Christ. The anticipation of the coming of Christ was manifestly strong in the church of the New Testament. The need to correct certain interpretations and attitudes

111

with reference to the anticipated *Parousia* is part of the New Testament record. What abides is that the church's hope continues to be in Christ, not only in that which He is now doing through the presence and ministry of His Holy Spirit, but also that which He will yet do in His final coming and ultimate victory over that which stands in the ways of God's redeeming love. Apart from Jesus Christ the church has no final hope.

THE MEDIATE HOPE: RENEWAL

To many in this generation, the biblical portrayal of the ultimate hope of the church seems so far removed from experience that it appears irrelevant. It is appropriate to ask then what are the more immediate prospects for the church? What is its hope for tomorrow?

The response to this question must be given in humility and caution. Though men of science are devoting themselves to serious study of the probable shape of life in this world in the next several decades, it is still generally recognized that we cannot know with precision or certainty what tomorrow will bring (Jas. 4:13-16). In its human dimension, the destiny of the church is very much tied up with the destiny of the world.

Focusing more directly, however, on the question of whether the organized church is likely to survive and whether Christianity will continue to be a dominant influence in the modern world, the responses to this question are varied but fall into two broad categories.

Prophets of Doom

There are prophets of doom both within the church and outside of it who say, "The church has had it." They do not see any probability that the church can be renewed in such measure that it will again become the kind of vital force in the world which it has been in the past. They foresee for the church a place of decreasing influence and the status of a shrinking minority in a growing world.

They point to the declining impact of the church on European and American social, political, and economic life. They point to the attitudes of many young people toward the organized church. They mention the defection of many ministers and priests from their responsibilities. They quote the statistics that the membership of the church is not growing as rapidly as the population of the world, thus making Christianity a smaller and smaller numerical minority. They list the failures of the church which were mentioned in the previous lesson as being responsible for the general lack of interest in what the church is concerned about.

They affirm that the world has come of age, that modern man no longer wants or needs what the church offers and that what we are witnessing is simply a further step in the emancipation of the masses from the mythologies and religions of the past, including Christianity. They affirm that we are living in a post-Christian era.

Prophets of Hope

There is, however, another point of view, an optimistic perspective. It is competently represented by Kenneth Scott Latourette, for many years Sterling Professor of Missions and Oriental History at Yale University. At the age of 83 he was still actively traveling through the world lecturing, teaching, and writing. In response to an interview conducted by editor Carl F. H. Henry of *Christianity Today,* he reflected a point of view quite other than that which is commonly expressed by the "prophets of doom."[3] In response to the question, "How do you calculate the impact of Christianity of Christ upon our generation?" he answered, "I am convinced that Christ has never been as widely and deeply influential in the world as He is today. First, because Christians— those who bear the Christian name—continue to grow in numbers. The global planting of Christianity in the nineteenth century was connected with western colonialism and imperialism, and one would expect that with the passing of colonialism and imperialism and the communist conquest of much of the world, these Christian churches would disappear. Exactly the contrary has happened. In no country, so far as I am aware, have Christians completely disappeared. They are still very strong in Russia."

He was also asked, "What do you think about the present state of American Christianity?" He answered, "I think it is still very vigorous. . . . The proportion of church members in this country has been mounting fairly steadily: about five out of a hundred when our nation became independent; about twelve out of a hundred at the time of the Civil War; about twenty-five out of a hundred at the turn of the century. Today—if you include Catholics, Protestants, Orthodox, and Jews, about two-thirds of the population call themselves members of a religious community— the vast majority of those being Christians."

Again he was asked, "Do you think the church has reason to lose heart because of the expansion of totalitarian communism?" To this he replied, "Surely not. She has survived dark hours in the past. Islam tore away about half of Christendom about A.D. 700, and the rest of Christendom was threatened partly by internal decay and partly by waves of barbarians sweeping down from the North. And we ought not to forget the condition of the church in fifteenth-century Europe." Later he added, "My guess is that Christianity will continue to be more deeply rooted in indigenous leadership and indigenous movements, and among more people and in more countries than any other religion has ever been. You see, Christianity today is more widely distributed geographically than any other religion has ever been. There is no exception to that among the major religions of mankind. . . . Christianity is not only more widely distributed; it's also more deeply rooted."

Signs of Hope

Latourette is not alone in his optimism concerning the future of the church. Others too point to developments which may be described as signs of hope:

1. The Whole Church in Mission
Throughout the churches, both Roman Catholic and Protestant, there is a new awareness that the mission of the church is the responsibility of "the whole people of God" rather than of an official few. This is sometimes called "the renewal of the laity."

114

While the impact of this is hard to measure and the implications of it may be hard to predict, it is surely one of the vital signs of life of the church. The possibility for a new powerful thrust of mission is tremendous.

2. Ministry to the Whole Person

There is a new awareness of the unitary character of man and the need to minister to him in his totality. This is to be recognized not only in the thinking of Christian leaders but it is also evident in the findings of the practice of modern medicine and the insights gained through the behavioral sciences. This is manifesting itself in many places in closer cooperation between those who represent the area of the spiritual and those who work with the physical and the emotional needs of men, between ministers, medical doctors, and psychiatrists.

3. Unity and Cooperation

There is a new spirit of unity among the churches which has developed particularly within this century. Although not all of the dimensions of the various ecumenical movement are necessarily to be considered of God, there can be no question but that in recent decades Christians are discovering each other as brethren in the faith. They are finding more ways in which they can work together and thus give a more united testimony in the world and serve with greater effectiveness. In the Mennonite brotherhood, too, considerable progress has been made in recent decades in the realization of true fellowship across denominational lines and in the achievement of true cooperation in common tasks. The Mennonite Central Committee and the Mennonite World Conference are two familiar illustrations of this.

4. Vigorous Young Churches

There are also new surges of life and growth of the church particularly in areas where the Christian faith has arrived more recently. Various areas in South America, Africa, and Asia report rapid growth. Some of this growth has come under the impact of the modern charismatic movements where the work of the Holy

Spirit receives special emphasis. Whenever such rapid growth occurs, it needs to be properly understood and interpreted. However, it is the occasion for rejoicing and is evidence that God continues to work in and through the church.

Donald R. Jacobs has made the significant observation that by now approximately one-fourth of the Mennonites of the world are nonwhite and that it is precisely this part of the brotherhood which is increasing at the most rapid rate. This is a sign of hope. It is also a stimulus and challenge to segments of the Mennonite brotherhood which are not growing.

IMPLICATIONS OF HOPE FOR THE CHURCH IN MISSION

An Alternative to Despair

Christian hope is the church's alternative to despair. In a world where men search for meaning and many fail to find it, where nihilism (a philosophy that human life is meaningless) is strong, where old values are rejected and new ones quickly prove inadequate, the temptation to despair is strong. While the technological possibilities before modern man are great, they may be developed for either good or evil purposes. We are told that man today has "unlimited powers for production" but also "unlimited powers for destruction."

The prospects before mankind externally are by no means reassuring. The continuing specter of devastating nuclear war, the agonizing power struggles between the races, and the possibility that the population explosion may lead soon to global poverty and famine are not simply imagined phobias. They are, humanly speaking, grim possibilities. In their presence some people give way to despair.

Not so, the church with its message and dynamic of hope. In the perspective of Christian hope, the church has an alternative to despair. History has meaning. It is moving toward a goal. The destiny of men and nations lies ultimately with God. We look for a new heaven and a new earth.

116

An Alternative to Revolution

Christian hope is also the church's alternative to revolution. The word *revolution* is here used in the popular sense of "social change through violence." Christian hope is an alternative to all other forms of hope which are either partially false or totally false. Various movements in the world offer men hope, but cannot ultimately deliver the goods.

Emil Brunner notes that Christian hope, itself revolutionary in character, is the end of other kinds of hope. He says,

> The revolutionary character of the Christian faith means: only the regenerate man can create truly new conditions. . . . The Christian faith revolutionizes the idea of revolution in that it perceives the only real revolution to be one which works from within outwards, and all others as mere camouflaged reaction. The contrast goes still deeper: the Christian faith sees true revolution to consist in the fact that man surrenders his claim to freedom and receives his true freedom from dependence on God. Only by men who recognize their freedom to lie in obedience and trust towards God can a new society, an order of justice and humanity, be built up. So-called revolutions which begin as an impulse toward freedom end always in a monstrous mass slavery and collectivism which robs man of his true human values.[4]

A Dynamic for Mission

To speak of Christian hope as offering an alternative to despair and an alternative to violent human revolution, does not mean that the church may then relax its efforts. In fact, it is by its involvement in mission that the church makes concrete its hope.

Jürgen Moltmann says, "The coming Lordship of the Risen Christ cannot be merely hoped for and awaited. This hope and expectation also sets its stamp on life, action, and suffering in the history of society. Hence mission means not merely propagation of faith and hope, but also historic transformation of life."[5] Hans Margull says, "Evangelism has been defined as 'hope in action.' The same definition holds true for the wider concept of mission.

Mission is hope in action. . . . Mission is defined only by our hope that God will have the last word in this world."[6]

Conceived in hope and sustained by hope, the church has courage to continue its task of mission. On the one hand, the church is always mindful that the kingdom of God is God's doing and God's gift. It does not come by human effort or in response to human merit. This helps to keep the church from presumption and pride in its achievements, or from anxiety and despair in its failures.

On the other hand, Christian hope serves as stimulus, as encouragement, and as direction for the wholehearted investment of the church's resources in mission. Freed from anxieties about its own survival, responding to the missionary mandate of its living Lord, sustained by the awareness of His abiding presence, and confident that one day the kingdom of this world will become the kingdom of the Lord and of His Christ (Rev. 11:15) the church may immerse itself completely in the task of witness and service. The church knows that as long as it remains obedient to the Lord, sensitive to the leading of the Holy Spirit, and speaking to the authentic needs of men, its ministry has meaning, not only in time, but for eternity.

> Therefore, my beloved brethren, be steadfast, immovable, always abounding in the work of the Lord, knowing that in the Lord your labor is not in vain. 1 Corinthians 15:58

1 Juergen Moltmann, *Theology of Hope* (New York: Harper and Row, 1967), p. 325.

2 Paul Erb, *The Alpha and the Omega* (Scottdale, Pennsylvania: Herald Press, 1955), p. 108.

3 Article in *Christianity Today*, October 13, 1967, pp. 6, 7. Copyright 1967 by *Christianity Today*; reprinted by permission.

4 From *Eternal Hope* by Emil Brunner, translated by Harold Knight. Published in the U.S.A. by The Westminster Press, 1954. Used by permission. Pp. 62, 63.

5 Moltmann, *op. cit.*, pp. 329, 330.

6 Hans Jochan Margull in Thomas Wieser, ed., *Planning for Mission* (New York: The U.S. Conference for the World Council of Churches, 1966), pp. 33, 34.

Erland Waltner is president of Mennonite Biblical Seminary, Elkhart, Indiana. He is a native of South Dakota. He received the AB degree from Bethel College, North Newton, Kansas; the STB from Biblical Seminary in New York; and the ThM and ThD from Eastern Baptist Theological Seminary in Philadelphia. He has also studied at the University of South Dakota, Temple University, and Princeton Theological Seminary.

He has served as a pastor and as a college and seminary professor. From 1956 to 1962 he was president of the General Conference Mennonite Church. He is currently the president of the Mennonite World Conference.